# Standards of Ministry

Jay Nembhard

All scripture quotes unless otherwise noted are from The New King James version, copyright (c) 1982, Thomas Nelson, Inc.

Copyright © 2014 Jay Nembhard

All rights reserved.

ISBN-13: 978-1505415674
ISBN-10: 1505415675

# CONTENTS

    FORWARD

1   THE STRUGGLE TO STAY RELEVANT   1

2   THE SPIRIT OF STANDARDS   7

3   HOLD YOUR HORSES   23

4   FAITHFULLY YOURS   37

5   SHOW ME AN EXAMPLE   47

6   LOOSE CANNONS AND TICKING TIME BOMBS   59

7   TITHING ME CRAZY   77

8   WHY NO WINE?   89

9   TV OR NOT TV?   109

10   WELCOME TO MY PARLOUR SAID THE SPIDER TO THE FLY   127

    ABOUT THE AUTHOR

# FOREWORD

The first time I really talked to Jay Nembhard was at the London, Walthamstow Conference in November 2005. In that large gathering of UK pastors, Jay was easy to remember because of his eager and assertive intellect chomping at the bit for a rigorous discussion. Being one who likes to mix it up a little bit, as well, Jay and I became fast friends.

Later, in the winter of 2006, I had the opportunity to preach for Jay in Wolverhampton. Every morning, along with pastors Marco Buzzella and Paul Boddy, we'd take refuge from the gray Easter days in a coffee shop spending hours sermonizing and parsing the scriptures like rabbis. Our roundtable was open, frank, and thought provoking.

It's in *this spirit* that Jay has written this book on standards. His motive is not to hold the rest of us to his personal dogmas about the meaning of righteousness but rather to quantify standards, practices, and "rules of thumb" that most of us have embraced since the earliest days of our conversions. There is no question that higher standards are indispensable to godly leadership but Jay takes it a step further by biblically walking us through the issues.

    This book should also become a "go to" manual for new pastors seeking to impart strong convictions to new converts. Exceptional chapters on faithfulness, media, drinking, tithing, and other important topics will save more than a few phone calls to busy overseeing pastors. Everything in here is practical and helpful to the everyday Christian life. And even Jay Nembhard will have a hard time arguing with that.

Fred Rubi,
Tucson, AZ

# 1. THE STRUGGLE TO STAY RELEVANT

Let it be known that every church denomination, organisation, group (whatever you want to call it) that had started out in blazing revival has ended up stone cold religious death. Without naming names if we all did a little research we will be shocked to find out just how tragic this really is. Churches that were exploding in the hundreds in a short space of time are now many years later closing down month after month with no sign of change or things turning around.

We would be arrogant fools if we feel that somehow we are unique. Spiritual decay will come to all unless we learn the lessons of the past. We live in a fallen world and things tend to fall apart if left alone. Throughout history we have seen, except for the rare occasion, a downward progression of the spirituality and effectiveness of a particular church or denomination.

Tragically it seems like the next generation fail to live up to the effectiveness of the previous generation. This has been true since time memorial. In that the old proverb is true – "The more things change, the more they remain the same."

This is what we see in Judges 2:10 which points out that *"When all that generation had been gathered to their fathers, another generation arose after them who did not know the Lord nor the work which He had done for Israel."* How many churches do we see today that are completely at odds with their inceptions? Today we have Methodist ministers not believing in hell, Baptist churches that have not baptised people in years, Pentecostal fellowships where people are not filled with the Holy Spirit, etc.

This book by no means is the remedy to spiritual decay. I claim no special knowledge in the ability to create and maintain revival. But I do know that one area that can truly help us to keep our lights bright from generation to generation is in the area of keeping our ministers spiritually effective. We will stay sharp if we can adhere to our standards of ministry.

(Note for the rest of the book, when I speak of ministers and ministries I am not talking about the pastoral role but ministries within the local church whether they be ushering, drama, nursery, bible study, etc.)

Thus purpose of this book is written to inform, to instruct and to remind members (and mainly ministers) of the Potter's House Christian Fellowship Church as to the standards of ministry as set out by our Fellowship. The purpose of this is to set out a clear light as what is expected of those who would volunteer their services to the local church.

Ministerial standards are all about church effectiveness (more in the next chapter). However, how we approach these ministry standards can either hinder or help our church. I would like to identify three potential pitfalls in maintaining these standards.

## UNCONSCIOUS NEGLECT

It is possible as the local church grows and ministries multiply, new converts can rise up in an atmosphere where standards, crucially implemented and enforced in the early days, are overlooked due to the busy pace of the church. As a result there is a downgrading of spiritual standards which, if not recognised and confronted, will result in the gradual decrease in effectiveness of the local church.

This gradual decrease in effectiveness becomes glaringly apparent as we continue to church plant. The time will come when the best of disciples from an era where ministry standards were upheld will be sent out and when that happens a veil will be lifted and we will be left in horror to see that the next generation are not as sharp or focused as the previous one. As a result of this our church becomes substandard and it is lot harder to disciple these men once they are set in their ways.

It is also possible for the older generation to lose its cutting edge as it sees the 'liberty' in which the new generation functions. Either way our church loses its ability to impact the world around us.

Unconscious neglect is the bane of effectiveness. That is why maintenance is such a critical aspect in life. Deflated tires and dirty sparkplugs cause a car to burn more fuel than is necessary. It is therefore useful once in a while to check the car over to make sure it runs at maximum efficiency. The same is true with the church and a book like this helps in making sure we are at our best. It is better to give ourselves to maintenance than to neglect the whole thing until it completely breaks down and then having to start from square one all over again.

## ZEAL WITHOUT KNOWLEDGE

Secondly, this book is written to make people understand the 'spirit' of ministry standards. This isn't just a book of dos and don'ts. This is written so that you understand why we do what we do. Obeying standards without understanding why can be legalism. We are not looking for robots, clones or 'yes men' but men and women of God who will be effective in the local church to bring honour and glory to Jesus Christ.

Failure to understand the 'why' of ministry can be as destructive as neglect. I have known 'firebrands for Jesus' in their zeal for the Fellowship have used standards as a means of beating people over the head. As soon as people step through the front door of the church standards are read out like the Riot Act.

Converts, barely saved from a concert, drama or service, are told in no uncertain terms what is expected of them now that they are saved. I can recall years ago when a young Michelle Douglas (who would become the wife of Pastor Kosi Amesu) came to church for the first time. She was seated next to an overzealous brother whose first sentence to her was "We don't allow women to preach in this church!"

Cinemas are out and televisions are to be thrown away. Fasting and all night prayer are in. Visitors are told in great boldness just how radical a church we are. I've known young pastors who are proud defenders of Fellowship standards. They've shown their zeal in the fact that there is no one in their churches as they have preached out every one of those lukewarm pseudo-saints. They're bringing out the heavy guns to show just how they mean business when it comes to standards. If you want to pass the offering bucket in church you better be in a three piece suit! Sigh.

There are reasons why we have standards and it isn't because we are gluttons for punishment or because we have a mission to make members of our churches amongst the most miserable people in the world. Every standard has a good reason and ultimately is for the purpose of keeping our churches effective and having impact in the world for Christ. If that standard wasn't needed, it would not be there. Simple!

If we can understand why we do what we do it would make living the standards far easier as we will then see them for our own good and effectiveness. It would also protect us from misunderstanding, misapplication and overzealous enthusiasts who would substitute rules for fruitfulness.

## ASSUMPTIONS

Thirdly, in order to get people to have a right perspective on ministry standards, in this book we will be looking at standards that are made very clear and standards that are assumed.

Notice that I did say 'assumed' because there are times we as a church expect things from people yet never really made it clear what we expected. The issue of television and personal faithfulness may be made clear but issues such as accountability or even alcohol were assumed. When 'violators' of these standards are brought to task there are those who won't buy the idea that they never knew. "You should have known we don't believe in drinking alcohol!" How were they to know if no one told them?

Assumption is just as deadly as neglect as it is possible to assume those in ministry are actually practising standards in their lives. We assume that they don't drink or that they are accountable to someone and so forth when they are not. When we finally find out that they are not functioning properly we get mad at them but how can we be mad with people who were never fully trained? How can we be upset with people we never communicated with properly?

Taking things for granted is a sure-fire way of creating misunderstanding and spiritual ignorance. What a tragedy to have believed for a long time that the church is going a certain way only to find out in shock months later that in fact it is going in the opposite direction.

In short, it is my prayer that this book will straighten out ideas and help us to observe the standards as shown that we may be effective ministers of Christ in these last days.

## 2. THE SPIRIT OF STANDARDS

One underlining theme of this book will be the theme of 'the spirit of the standards'. As I have said in the previous chapter, the whole reason behind standards is to make the church as effective as it can be. With godly standards working, the local church can have more impact and make the most of the talents and gifts that God has equipped her with. Without standards, the church is only in first gear and unable to capitalise on the opportunities that would come her way.

### THE PURPOSE OF STANDARDS IS FOR EFFECTIVENESS

While pioneering in Manchester many years ago it hit me that the main tragedies affecting the church world wasn't just churches closing down but also churches with some semblance of life not maximising the potential they had within. It would sadden me to see churches filled with gifted youth accomplish nothing in their local community and the world around them.

This tragedy is nothing new. The apostle Paul deals

with such a church in 1 Corinthians 10:23 when he said, *"All things are lawful for me, but not all things are helpful; all things are lawful for me, but not all things edify."* There were Christians in the Corinthian church bragging on the fact that they were free to do as they liked as Christians. Paul points out that although that may be true, freedom doesn't necessarily help the Christian or build them up!

In order to be effective, freedom at times may have to be restricted. You ask any world class athlete if they are free to eat junk food, sleep in late and not train and they will tell you "yes". But they will also tell you that if they don't discipline themselves and enforce certain standards in their lives they will never be world or Olympic champions.

I can guarantee you that Britain (or any other nation for that matter) will not allow an athlete to represent them at the Olympic games if they have not imposed certain standards upon themselves in order to have impact on those games. Yet Christians have a problem when a church imposes standards upon those who wish to participate when in reality all the church wants is to have impact in the world.

## GOING BEYOND THE INTENDED PURPOSE

In saying all of that however, there lies a great danger in having standards. It is very possible where we elevate standards beyond what it was intended. The problem with our corrupt human nature is that we often times take something good and make a disaster out of it.

During the time of Moses, the Israelites complained against God for taking them out of Egypt. Fiery serpents were sent to bring judgment upon these ungrateful people. As they cried out in repentance God told Moses to build a bronze serpent. Numbers 21:8-9 states, *"Then the Lord said* to Moses, *"Make a fiery serpent, and set it on a pole; and it shall be that everyone who is bitten, when he looks at it, shall live." So Moses made a bronze serpent, and put it on a pole; and so it was, if a serpent had bitten anyone, when he looked at the bronze serpent, he lived."*

Fantastic! Problem solved! But that's not the end of the story. The Israelites were so delighted with the bronze serpent that they ended up worshipping it and so in the end it had to be destroyed. 2 Kings 18:4 states, *"He [Hezekiah] removed the high places and broke the sacred pillars, cut down the wooden image and broke in pieces the bronze serpent that Moses had made; for until those days the children of Israel burned incense to it, and called it Nehushtan."* The purpose of the bronze serpent was to bring healing. It was not to be worshipped!

Human nature has not changed. When it comes to standards, something that was initially meant to bring edification to the church can become the very death of it! What I mean is that standards become something that it was never meant to be and the good it initially brought can turn to harm.

Take for example the Amish. There is a reason why Amish men wear beards without moustaches. Back in the 1700s soldiers wore moustaches and because the Amish wanted to be seen as men of peace and not men of war they refused to wear moustaches.

But that was over 300 years ago and things have drastically changed. But to an Amish person, wearing a moustache is worldly! So now a standard that was meant to reflect peacefulness has become a necessary identification of what a true Christian should look like.

This is not simply an Amish problem but Christianity throughout the centuries where standards that initially meant something have lost its meaning over the years and has become the cornerstone of that particular denomination's identity. Why they do what they do is a mystery to them but they are loyal to it and that's what counts! If anyone questions the logic of such a standard they are viewed as disloyal to their traditions. I have known of a young man who went to visit a church in Manchester only to be thrown out for having long hair!

While traditions have value (2 Thessalonians 2:15; 1 Corinthians 11:2; Proverbs 22:28) we must also understand the purpose for which they are intended. It is very possible to be doing something that has nothing to do with the effectiveness or spiritual uplifting of the church.

Back in 1986, WBC world super-featherweight champion Julio Cesar Chavez from Mexico was moving up in weight and challenging the WBA world lightweight champion Edwin Rosario from Puerto Rico. Chavez at that time was unbeaten in over fifty fights and was a serious threat to Rosario.

As a result, Rosario hired a witch doctor to curse Chavez. Chavez heard about this and believing this stuff got himself a witch doctor as well who told him that if he wore a red ribbon around his head as he gets into the ring he would be protected from Rosario's curses. Chavez did what he was told and knocked out Rosario in the eleventh.

Chavez being cursed is not the issue. The issue is that he wore that red ribbon for the purpose of warding off curses. Ever since then many Mexican fighters come into the ring wearing the red ribbon emulating Julio Cesar Chavez. But if you were to ask them for what the purpose they have no idea. They are just doing what Chavez used to do. But the purpose was to ward off witchcraft and for most no one had threatened them with sorcery! This is where tradition loses its effectiveness and becomes something people do just because others do it. That red ribbon has lost its meaning!

## STANDARDS VERSUS SALVATION

It becomes a bigger problem when these same standards subtly become the means of salvation! Ephesians 2:8-9 tells us that *"For by grace you have been saved through faith, and that not of yourselves; it is the gift of God, not of works, lest anyone should boast. For we are His workmanship, created in Christ Jesus for good works, which God prepared beforehand that we should walk in them."* In other words, the works we accomplish do not create our salvation but is rather an outflow of our salvation. Our works do not save us but simply show that we are saved.

We need to remember this, especially when it comes to standards. We have some fantastic standards that have been implemented to bring personal and corporate effectiveness. But there are many who are spiritually immature who even realising it elevate those standards to the criterion of salvation.

Paul reminds us of this because our natural disposition is bent towards a list of do's and don'ts that when accomplished assures us of salvation. For some people the idea of salvation is linked to church attendance, the length of one's hair, long dresses and shirts with long sleeves! They have not realised that over the years, the standard of membership, has slowly evolved to become the litmus test for salvation!

It's a known fact that if a young Christian lady goes to a traditional Pentecostal-Holiness church without a hat she is seen as unsaved and worldly. If her hair is braided or makeup, or worse, if she wears trousers, she is the second coming of Jezebel!

It is one thing to have a standard of how a woman should dress but to make it a condition of salvation is something different.

As history goes, old churches with old traditional standards of salvation gives way to newer churches with still new traditional standards of salvation. We may not view a young lady as unsaved with braided hair, makeup and jewellery but what if someone who attends our church has a television? Or worse still, goes to the cinema!

I have seen on a number of occasions in my own church people reading new converts the riot act in regards to television, cinema, church attendance and the like. Somehow standards that are meant for ministry saints are seen by so-called established members as standards of salvation that are applicable to everyone that steps through the church door.

It is disturbing to hear established members talk about certain Christians, viewing them as not truly saved, not because of issues such as fornication, adultery, drunkenness or other related things but because they have a DVD player or because they don't go to a mid-week service. It's a dangerous thing when we in presumption make our standards the requirements of salvation.

## A POSSIBLE SOURCE OF PRIDE

The other danger about standards is that because many other churches have none or too few we can begin to view ourselves as their betters. I remember coming to church and some old loon telling me that *"There is saved and there is Potter's House saved"*. Really? Where is that in the Bible? It's like saying, *"There is pregnancy and then there is Potter's House pregnancy."* How pregnant is pregnant? How saved is saved? This is a very dangerous place to be in because pride will lead to destruction (Proverbs 16:18).

John Alexander Dowie, a preacher used greatly by God to bring back the healing ministry into mainstream Christianity back in the late 1800s began proclaiming himself Elijah because he looked around and saw that no one was doing what he was doing. As a result of this self-exaltation he ruined his ministry and became a laughing stock.

It was the Church of Christ, I believe, who back in the early 1800s formed with the sincere desire to be completely right with God. After a while they began to believe that no one was living for God like they were and that everyone else were compromisers. Eventually they came to believe that they were the only true Church and everyone else apostate with their church standards elevated to the level of salvation.

This is a denomination that ever since has had more splinters than a 2' x 4' as various churches and members argue over the slightest thing and making them major issues.

Contentions in the Church of Christ have taken place over the communion cup. One group said that one cup should be used for everyone while another group said that small cups should be used by individuals. As a result the Church of Christ has split into the one-cuppers and the multi-cuppers with each one saying that the other one is not really saved.

Then there was the argument over music. Should musical instruments be used in the house of God? One group said "yes" and another said "no" and once again as a result you have the instrumental Church of Christ and the non-instrumental Church of Christ with each one saying the other is not right with God.

There was also the disagreement over Sunday

school. One group believed it to be unbiblical and the other believing it to be of God. Once again there was the inevitable split with those having a Sunday school to be seen by their opposite side as inspired of Satan.

(I wonder if there is such a thing as a one-cupper, musical instrument, non-Sunday school, pre-millennial Church of Christ or a multi-cup, non-musical instrument, Sunday school, post-millennial Church of Christ.)

Salvation is through Christ and Him alone. Standards may make us more effective but it doesn't make us any more saved. A woman is either pregnant or not pregnant. We are either saved or not saved. Pride and arrogance makes us think that we are more saved because of our standards and not because of the finished work of Christ.

## STANDARDS VERSUS LEGALISM

If we haven't got a right understanding of standards we do more harm than help. Jesus said in Mark 2:22, "*...no one puts new wine into old wineskins; or else the new wine bursts the wineskins, the wine is spilled, and the wineskins are ruined. But new wine must be put into new wineskins.*" In the old days, wineskins were made out of fresh animal leather. There was a reason for this. New wine ferments and in so doing generates gas and heat. Because the wineskin is new it is able to expand and take the heat without breaking. But an old wineskin has become 'set' and so is unable to expand and take the heat. So if new wine is put into an old wineskin the result is that the wineskin cracks and the wine leaks out. So both wine and wineskin is ruined.

The answer is to put new wine into new wineskin as the wineskin can take the gas and heat and so both are preserved and to put old wine into old wineskin because the old wine will not continue to ferment and so the old wineskin doesn't need to expand.

The idea of this parable is do not put a new Christian and try and contain them into a system that older Christians are already used to. I have learned to fast for a week at a time but it took me over fifteen years of salvation before I did it. I have outreached in the cold and snow for a whole day but I was saved for a while before I did it.

Imagine me imposing these rules on someone who just became a Christian the day before? New Christians (new wine) can't handle the restrictions. It would destroy the new convert and it would make the life I live seem draconian and put people off Christianity.

The amazing thing in church is that I give new converts the grace and patience needed to grow as Christians yet when those same new converts get established they exhibit none of those graces on the next generation of new converts.

It took them months to stop smoking cigarettes but they are demanding new converts saved a week to stop smoking. I have seen young ladies who got saved come to church initially in very short skirts yet years later a new convert can come in dressed very similar and she is viewed as a Jezebel.

So it is very possible that we can get to a place where a good thing like standards becomes an ugly thing called legalism because we can forget it took us a while to get into the mode of discipline that we now view as standard living. How easily saints, forgetful of their past, can implement and enforce standards on the new convert, something no one did to them.

Legalism is not only a distinct possibility but it is almost guaranteed if church members who have embraced standards do not understand them for themselves. The reason it is a distinct possibility is sadly many Christians are lazy in their thinking and do not like to think things through.

## FLEXIBLE STANDARDS AND INFLEXIBLE LEGALISM

The reason why it is so easy to be legalistic is that all it takes is the acceptance of certain rules and regulations. People love to think in black and white because it is far easier than thinking things through. Without the ability to think things through it means Christians are likely to be inflexible when it comes to working with standards.

A good case in point was a few years ago when Mel Gibson's film "The Passion of the Christ" came out. It was a powerful demonstration of Christ and the brutality of His suffering and death that facilitated for us salvation and the forgiveness of sin. This was literally a God-send as this powerful demonstration could be used to reach sinners in a way we never had before.

This film had generated so much interest because of its controversial nature. As a result it was felt that here was a one in a lifetime opportunity to reach people that could not be missed. Therefore our elders made the decision, as a one-off, for us to attend the cinema as a church and invite as many sinners as we could to see this film in the hope that they would get saved.

Instantly there were those who protested at the 'hypocrisy'. In their words they felt that we can't just pick and choose when to go and when not to go to the cinema. If it is wrong to go before then it was wrong to go for the film. If we are now allowed to go to see this film then we should abandon the standard of banning cinema attendance.

I always wondered if these people could not just think that God never called us to be slaves to standards. The whole purpose of standards is for spiritual impact. Here was a one-off, once in a lifetime opportunity to reach sinners and yet there were those who could not see the forest for the trees. They could not see beyond the black and white standards and see that there was a greater good being done.

Jesus was no slave to standards. It was He who said in Matthew 5:17-18, *"Do not think that I came to destroy the Law or the Prophets. I did not come to destroy but to fulfil."* Yet when it came to the greater good He was willing that the Law be put aside.

There are two simultaneous examples of this in the gospel of Luke.

Luke 6:1-11 states, *"***1** *Now it happened on the second Sabbath after the first that He went through the grainfields. And His disciples plucked the heads of grain and ate them, rubbing them in their hands.* **2** *And some of the Pharisees said to them, "Why are you doing what is not lawful to do on the Sabbath?"* **3** *But Jesus answering them said, "Have you not even read this, what David did when he was hungry, he and those who were with him:* **4** *how he went into the house of God, took and ate the showbread, and also gave some to those with him, which is not lawful for any but the priests to eat?"* **5** *And He said to them, "The Son of Man is also Lord of the Sabbath."* **6** *Now it happened on another Sabbath, also, that He entered the synagogue and taught. And a man was there whose right hand was withered.* **7** *So the scribes and Pharisees watched Him closely, whether He would heal on the Sabbath, that they might find an accusation against Him.* **8** *But He knew their thoughts,* *and said to the man who had the withered hand, "Arise and stand here." And he arose and stood.* **9** *Then Jesus said to them, "I will ask you one thing: Is it lawful on the Sabbath to do good or to do evil, to save life or to destroy?"* **10** *And when He had looked around at them all, He said to the man, "Stretch out your hand." And he did so, and his hand was restored as whole as the other.* **11** *But they were filled with rage, and discussed with one another what they might do to Jesus."*

In both these cases we read of Jesus putting the needs of people ahead of the Law. Strict adherence to the Sabbath came secondary to a person's need for food and their need for healing. Doing what was right and helpful to one's fellow man had a greater priority than slavishly following a Law that was initially meant to help man by entitling him to a day of rest!

Think about it! We live in a mad rushing fast paced world. We are forever zipping and prancing here, there and everywhere. If you left it to people they would be active for every day of the week non-stop and ultimately burn themselves out. This is what we see in the world today...a world that is stressed out because of all that whizzing all over the place.

The idea of the Sabbath was for man to take a day out each week to rest, refresh, meditate, remember God and spend time with friends & family. It was made into a law so that the people of God had to respect it. That law was made for the spiritual wellbeing of the individual by giving him rest.

But these Pharisees had so slavishly followed the law they just didn't get it. So when they rebuked Jesus for allowing His disciples to eat the heads of grain they were in effect saying that rubbing the heads of grain to eat constitutes work and working on the Sabbath is forbidden because we are to rest and not to work.

Yes, that was true in black and white but when you look at it closer, remembering that the spirit of the Law was meant to help people, you will see that they were in effect really saying that they should stay hungry on a day that was designed to help the disciples restore and replenish themselves! In other words, by telling the disciples not to eat ran counter to the whole purpose of that Law which was to revitalise men. They were really saying, *"You are not to eat but to stay hungry because this is a day of rest and revitalisation."* How absurd!

But because of their black and white thinking they couldn't see that they were talking absurdities. That is how people are who follow the standards without thinking things through.

The whole idea of standards is for us to have impact. By relaxing the standard of cinema for the case of "The Passion of the Christ" caused us to have impact. If we had followed the letter of the law we would have missed a golden opportunity of reaching thousands for Jesus worldwide. We would have lost out because we did not understand the spirit of the standard. It was not an excuse for people to now to have Saturday night fellowships at the Ritz.

I have given this example because now and again there may be, due to some extreme circumstance, a standard or way in which we do things that has to be temporarily overlooked because of the greater good. If God can do that with His own Law then we most certainly can with our own standards.

It would be great if we could all understand 'the spirit of the standard' which is for us to have impact rather than just seeing the standard from a black and white point of view. You have some with the mindset, "We do this because this is what we do." That is just tragic.

Limited flexibility every now and again is not us abolishing standards or contradicting our stance but it is for the wellbeing of every individual and for the long term impact of the church. If we are going to be ministers helping to create a balanced church we need to remember this and that at times we have to 'play things by ear' just like Jesus did.

## STANDARDS DO NOT MAKE SAINTS

In closing, another reason why we need to remember 'the spirit of the standard' is that Christianity is a relationship with God and not a religion. Religion is all about external rules and regulations whereas a relationship is all about the internal heart of man.

The thing about standards and rules is that you can become so good at them and externally be without flaw. You can have an excellent disciple who has no television, who is always faithful in church attendance, who dresses very smart, who is on outreach, involved in various ministries and is faithful to his wife and a blessing to his pastor.

Yet he has no real prayer life as he only prays on the Monday night prayer meeting with the rest of his group. He does not read the bible except for his bible study group on Fridays or for the occasional sermon he preaches. It's not that he never did those things but over a period of time he has become so used to his EXTERNAL PERFORMANCE that he lost interest in his INTERNAL DEVOTION.

I have personally met men like this and it always amazes me how good a performer these disciples are. They are living embodiment of standards kept yet their heart is far from God.

They have lost the plot. The idea of standards is not so that other people can see our performance but for us to strengthen our own spiritual life with God. But the reality is that it is far easier to keep up a performance than get one's own heart right with God.

The rich young ruler from the gospel of Mark is a classic example.

Mark 10:17-22 tells us, "*17 Now as He was going out on the road, one came running, knelt before Him, and asked Him, "Good Teacher, what shall I do that I may inherit eternal life?" 18 So Jesus said to him, "Why do you call Me good? No one is good but One, that is, God. 19 You know the commandments: 'Do not commit adultery,' 'Do not murder,' 'Do not steal,' 'Do not bear false witness,' 'Do not defraud,' 'Honor your father and your mother.'" 20 And he answered and said to Him, "Teacher, all these things I have kept from my youth." 21 Then Jesus, looking at him, loved him, and said to him, "One thing you lack: Go your way, sell whatever you have and give to the poor, and you will have treasure in heaven; and come, take up the cross, and follow Me." 22 But he was sad at this word, and went away sorrowful, for he had great possessions.*"

When it came to keeping the standards of the Law, this young man was blameless. Externally he was a man without flaw or fault. But Jesus switches the argument and began to deal with the inside and on the inside we find something different. We find a man who loves money more than the will of God for his life and he would not give up his money for God.

I give this young man kudos however for the fact that although he tried his best to be externally right he knew in his heart something was wrong. He may not have known what but he knew that he lacked something.

How many upstanding people in our church know that they lack something? As militant as some of our standards are, it is far easier to conform these externalities than it is to deal with internal issues.

But if we can remember that the whole idea is 'the spirit of the standard', that is, all about spiritual effectiveness and impact then we should be able to face ourselves and try to measure up to that which we are trying to accomplish from the inside.

# 3. HOLD YOUR HORSES

STANDARDS OF MINISTRY. What does this actually mean? Over the years I have seen Christians from other churches look in puzzlement when hearing these words. It is an alien concept to some and I have known of Christians to act in mild surprise when they hear that in the Potter's House churches there are requirements necessary before someone can enter some sort of service in the church. Indeed, some think it strange that any church would have a set of conditions directed to those who would serve in their local church.

## STANDARDS: A NORMAL CHURCH REQUIREMENT

Yet this is nothing new. Conditions, requirements, standards, etc are nothing new to church life. As a matter of fact, not too long ago churches required attendees to adhere to a set of rules and regulations if they were to be considered members.

Some of these requirements were a bit farfetched. There were churches that scrutinised converts to see if they really were converts and put through a battery of tests before they got baptised and accepted in the local church and put on the membership roll.

Some churches required beards to be worn at all time while others viewed that moustaches were of the world and should be shaved regularly. Then there was the avoidance of pork and can you believe it...the avoidance of coffee, tea, Coca-Cola (they contain caffeine, a 'narcotic'). In some churches women could not wear makeup or jewellery or wear trousers!

But in general, in normal churches, the requirements were biblical in origin, e.g. tithing, an anti drug and alcohol stance, baptism, faithful church attendance, etc. And these were needed in order to bring about the stability and spiritual identity of that church. These requirements, for lack of a better word, were religiously followed and were held dear by the members of the church who felt it their God-given duty to uphold the distinctive of that church.

These practises have since been consigned to the history books and seen as outdated, not because we have 'evolved' into a stronger form of Christianity but the opposite. In times gone by, church attendance was the norm for most people. All across Britain church bells rang, churches of all denominations were filled with believers and the hymns of worshippers could be heard all through the land. The Monday morning newspapers had transcripts of sermons preached by popular preachers the day before. The role of a pastor was highly regarded and the word of God respected.

# BACKSLIDING BRITAIN AND THE LOSS OF STANDARDS

In today's Britain Christianity has regressed; relegated behind Islam, a foreign religion to this nation half a century ago yet given preferential treatment today. Church bells ring no more and grand looking church buildings lie empty, crumbling or sold as warehouses and apartment blocks. Many remaining churches are filled with old people who will be dead in a few years and when they go so too will the church.

The last newspaper that I know of to print a sermon transcript was the Times. However, it has been nearly a decade since it last published its 'Preacher of the Year' competition and with it, the winning sermon.

Today, the word of God is despised, ignored or viewed as a myth and a pastor is seen as a non-entity. Recently I applied for a bank account with a large high street bank. When asked for a job title I told them 'minister of religion' only to get a blank look as there was nothing on the system for a minister of religion. I was therefore confined to the ignobility of 'Other'.

So, what does this have to do with ministry? In the old days, since church attendance was the norm for most people, the church could impose regulations for church membership and ministry but in this day and age where church attendance is sparse and many churches are barely keeping their doors open, 'imposing' regulations is seen as suicidal. In today's church, we are just so happy that someone came through the door.

In my early days in Manchester I remember visiting a local church one Sunday evening (we didn't have an evening service then) only to find out that the praise and worship team, for whatever reason, did not show up that night. After about a twenty minute delay the pastor began to plead with the congregation for someone, anyone to play an instrument. *"Is there anyone here who can play the drums or keyboard and help us out?"* It was embarrassing to see a church minister grovel for help. It was embarrassing to see a church impotent in her service. It was embarrassing to see the pastor and a church elder left in the lurch by their worship team and forced to sing a cappella with croaky voices. It was embarrassing because it reinforced the world's idea of the church being useless.

This is no isolated incident and there are many churches across Britain who are literally begging for help. If churches are desperate for people to come through the doors how much more desperate are they for people to minister? Beggars, it is said, can't be choosers. This means that as long as someone has a talent or ability then in many cases no questions are asked. These churches are just so grateful that they have someone who can play an instrument, sing or work with their youth. Nothing is required of them except their talent. Nothing is asked about their character, spiritual depth, church background, doctrine, morals, convictions, etc. All that matters is that they can do a job for the church.

Around January 1999, again in the early days of pioneering in Manchester, I remember working with a troubled young man from a broken home. He was about nineteen years of age, living in a hostel, suffering from drink and drug problems and had confessed to me that he was sexually abused as a young boy and as a result was struggling with homosexual tendencies. After a few weeks of coming to church he disappeared without a trace. A few months went by before I received a telephone call from him. He had moved to Crewe, about thirty miles south-west of Manchester, found a church and within two weeks had become the youth leader of that church. This was a young man who barely knew Jesus, had all kinds of issues and now he's working with the youth. He was completely unqualified.

In time gone by he would have been clearly told to sit down for a while and let Jesus deliver him from all of his issues but in today's generation where we are so desperate, his tremendous need was not seen as today's church is so obsessed with its own need to survive that it cannot see the needs of those who God has brought in for them to help.

As difficult as it is to have a functioning church and as pressurising as it is to make something happen, it is ultimately a defeated strategy when you put the church's need to have people before the people's need to be made whole in Jesus.

No one in their right minds want to preach to empty chairs and we can be tempted to leave people as they are just so we can have the appearance of something happening. But broken down people can't be the means by which we build the foundation of the church because they are not whole and therefore not stable.

If they have not had a real encounter with Christ, if Christ has not healed them then it is only a matter of time before they fall away and you find yourself trading one person for the next and that is no way to build the church of God. It is a defeated strategy because all you are doing is trading the future where saints made whole by Jesus are ministering effectively for a present where it looks like something is taking place but it is more like the fizz in a glass of Coca-Cola.

# SWIMMING AGAINST THE CURRENT...IT'S WHAT LIVING FISH DO

Thus ministry in the Potter's House starts when we recognise the fact that we cannot afford to be desperate for either members or ministers. If we lose sight of the Church's purpose to make converts and disciples for Christ we will be like those unfortunate churches who are simply looking for church attendees in order to survive. We are not here for survival. We are here to build a long and lasting work.

It all starts by having a clear conviction that we are building a church with a solid foundation and like any true foundation we firstly have to dig down and dig deep before we build upwards. Thus standards are there for the purpose of pruning, that is, filtering out those who unqualified for ministry, e.g. unsaved people, those that are not committed to the ideals and vision of our church and those not qualified to lead.

So our first standard in regards to ministry is this. Every individual who desires to be involved in specialised church ministry has to be a regular attendee of the church for a minimum period of six months.

(When I speak of specialised church ministry I'm speaking of ministries such as platform ministry, Sunday school, ushering and so on as opposed to general church activities like outreaching, impact teams, attending prayer meetings, and so on.)

This six month minimum period is a time of evaluation in which individuals are assessed to see if they are worthy and capable of performing in the ministry that they desire to be in. This is why it is a minimum of six months because there is no guarantee that after six months an individual is ready to entire a particular ministry. It also gives those interested in ministry an opportunity to observe rather than rushing into something they may not have the commitment level for.

Like I said before, we are not begging anyone to enter any ministry no matter how desperate the need. It may seem like lunacy but we are looking at the bigger picture here. Once again, if we put our desperation above a person's qualification it will hurt the church in the long run.

To give in to desperation is to give out a wrong message. It tells everyone that ministry is not a privilege to be valued but simply doing the church a favour whenever we feel like it. Any church that wants to have impact in its community cannot be held to ransom by the whims of talented individuals. But we will look at this in depth in a later chapter.

## SALVATION IS A MUST

In that minimum period of six months we are looking for true conversion in men and women. You'd be amazed at just how many people are in ministry in their local church and they are not even converted to Christ! Just because someone does something for Jesus and are in church doesn't mean that they are saved. This is whether they go to the Potter's House or not!

The Lord Jesus said in Matthew 7:21-23, *""Not everyone who says to Me, 'Lord, Lord,' shall enter the kingdom of heaven, but he who does the will of My Father in heaven. Many will say to Me in that day, 'Lord, Lord, have we not prophesied in Your name, cast out demons in Your name, and done many wonders in Your name?' And then I will declare to them, 'I never knew you; depart from Me, you who practice lawlessness!'"*

Out of His own mouth Christ spoke of church people doing activities in the name of Jesus yet are not saved and right with God. I remember years ago Pastor Peter Ajala telling me of a time when he was invited to preach at a particular church's concert in Bristol. After preaching the altar call and giving the invitation to get saved, the entire choir of thirty plus people bar one came out of their seats to pray the sinner's prayer!

Now I don't know the hearts of the individuals that made up the choir. Maybe they were not used to such confrontational preaching or maybe they were struggling with issues but out of that thirty plus people I would dare say that there were some who were not right with God.

Being in a church like ours where we are straight up when it comes to bible truth it is more than likely that we will be able to see if someone is truly converted to Christ within that six month period. Real salvation means a change in character which is something we can observe over a six month period. People once on drugs have given them up, alcohol is rejected, bad language is no more and not just the negative but there is an inward desire for holiness, to live for God, prayer, reading the word of God, coming to church, etc. Six months is a fair enough time to see a transformation, a true inner change in the life of an individual.

## SPIRITUAL GROWTH IS A NECESSITY

But the assessment doesn't stop with conversion. One great thing about the six month period is that it is a time when a new Christian is left to grow and mature. Their personal relationship with God is the absolute priority. During this time the new convert learns the importance of church attendance, prayer, fasting, fellowship, reading the bible and so on as the means by which he or she focuses on Christ and so becomes spiritually nourished or 'recharged'. By being left alone for this period of time without the pressure of ministry he or she develops a habit of a lifetime which is of the upmost importance in keeping the spiritual life functioning.

Ministry, as important as it is, can be a distraction and draining. If a new Christian is given ministry without learning to focus on Christ then ministry will become the focus and not Christ. Thus ministry becomes a distraction and without Christ being the focus He cannot be their source of light and power. In other words, if a new convert has not mastered the habits of prayer, bible reading and other things that keeps the Christian fixed on Jesus and spiritually 'recharged' then ministry will cause them to drain away spiritually.

It will be only a matter of time before they drain out completely as their initial 'charge' is due to their new convert zeal but without a means of recharge they will become 'flat'. I would liken it to a mobile phone that is charged only once but if it is not connected to the charger it will no longer be of use once it is used completely.

I have known people over the years who have been faithful to their ministry but completely woeful when it came to their prayer life, personal devotion, reading of God's word and other means by which God uses to keep the spiritual life 'charged'. It was only a matter of time before these Christians fell completely. If that is true for older saints how much more true for new converts.

A number of years ago there was a revival of conversions amongst many of Jamaica's popular musicians. Individuals like Papa San, Lt. Stitchie, Judy Mowatt and so on were getting saved and becoming prominent Christian artistes. This revival produced a surprising convert in Desmond "Ninja Man" Ballentine. This was a great coup for the Jamaican Church.

Instant pressure was put on Ninja Man to perform as a Christian which he did for a while. But because he was never given enough time to grow in Christ, Ninja Man fell away and became the gangster he was before. Today he is in jail awaiting trial for murder.

There may be a number of factors when it came to his falling away but you can be sure that Ninja Man was not given a fair chance of survival because of severe distraction, distraction caused by the Church. So instead of giving the Jamaican Church a boost, this fiasco served to bring her reproach as the Church was now viewed as powerless to sustain Ninja Man in the faith.

Responsibility is a good thing and we all need it. But responsibility before spiritual maturity will cause young Christians to break down. Here are young fledglings doing their best to stay saved and keep their heads above water and now they are weighted down with ministerial responsibilities. This is overwhelming even for the most zealous and gifted of young believers.

Everyone deserves a good childhood. Every child needs that early period of their life where they are the centre of attention, where they are loved and looked after. Early childhood is that one period of their lives when it is absolutely necessary for them to be 'selfish', that is, take, take, take. It is completely natural for a baby to wake their parents at night demanding to be fed or changed. It is completely unnatural for a parent to leave that baby to fend for itself at such a tender age or to be involved in daily chores with the rest of the family. Not only is it unnatural, it is child abuse. No infant can live up to such responsibility.

If that child is left to develop naturally it is well on its way to becoming a well balanced adult who in the future contributes to society. In other words, having a good childhood is critical if one is to have a productive adulthood.

In our churches, it doesn't matter if you are Michael Jackson, Britney Spears, Beyoncé, Eminem or whoever. If you get saved you are going to sit down for six months in our congregation and take time to grow in Jesus and if after six months you still aren't ready you will have to sit down for however long it takes until you are ready spiritually. We are not looking for performers. We are looking for ministers. We are not making one hit wonders. We are making disciples of Christ who will stand the test of time.

## THE SPIRIT OF THE STANDARD

So we can see that the 'standard' implemented of a six month wait before entering into ministry is mainly for the spiritual health of the new convert. This is the SPIRIT of the standard. I have emphasised the word 'spirit' and will continue to do so throughout this book because of the danger we face of individuals hijacking the standard by focusing on the letter of the standard and not the spirit.

What I mean is there are people who just don't get why we do what we do. They hear about the six month waiting period and it becomes equal to the Ten Commandments and a cardinal sin if broken. So if a new convert gets saved on the 1st of January then he or she is not entitled to any ministry until the 1st of July. If it happens that an event is happening on the 30th of June that desperately needs new ministers then we just have to do the best that we can because that new convert can only minister 24 hours from now.

Think, man! Think! Is something magical going to happen in 24 hours where that new convert all of a sudden becomes qualified? How different will that new convert be in spiritual maturity 24 hours from now? The spirit of the standard is the spiritual wellbeing of that new convert, not the length of time they are in church. Some people mature faster than the average and some less. Just because someone has been in church for six months doesn't mean that they are now entitled to ministry either. Each person has to be judged by their own merit.

I have heard of young pastors who will not let a new convert pass the offering bucket around because he's not been saved six months. Then there are those who view the overhead projector as such a serious ministry that that young sister has to be in church for over six months before she can handle such a 'heavy' responsibility.

## MINISTRY AND NON-POTTER'S HOUSE CONVERTS

In closing, I would also like to make it clear in regards to people joining our Fellowship from another church. Though our ministry is particularly to reaching sinners and converting them to Christ, it has been my privilege to meet a number of good people who have joined and added to our church. These are usually people moving from another city or in a rare case from a church that was going through moral issues. I also add to the fact that I was also saved for eight months before joining the Potter's House.

Yet, unfortunately, I have had more bad encounters with people coming in from other churches than I have had good encounters. I have met people who have failed to see the irony of them trying to make my church a replica of their old one. If their old one was any good why did you leave it in the first place? And if the old one is bad why are you trying to make mine like yours?

Unfortunately there are many Christians out there looking for a church in order to have expression. They have no intention of partnering with the church but they are simply looking out for their own interests. They have no intention of submitting to the church's authority or obey her doctrines and traditions. All they are interested in is some type of ministry that they would be given expression in. This can be a real plague on the church where you have a rogue minister trying to use his or her position to infect new converts with rebellion and false doctrine and ultimately cripple or paralyse the church's influence.

People come to church for different reasons. Many are the motives of attendees. Some come for peace, others for a relationship or the blessing of God, the list is endless. While some motives may be harmless or at the worse hurt the individual themselves, there are those whose motives will hinder the effectiveness of the church.

For some people, especially from a church background, a period of longer than six months may be needed in order to protect the church. We need to know if they believe the same things that we do, if they are accountable and teachable, if they are a danger to others, are they filled with false doctrine, etc.

We have a responsibility to protect the members of our church. It would be ludicrous for a suspected wolf to be given sanctuary in the midst of a flock of sheep. I wish that everyone had only sincere motives for joining a church but that is sadly not the case. And for the sake of the flock, every new Christian has to be examined to see if they will be a blessing or a hindrance to the Church. Once someone has been given ministry they would have automatically received credibility as well. Taking back the ministry and credibility is a lot harder than giving it.

It is better to be safe than sorry. It is better to wait than rush. Yes, short term gains can be acquired but that can be followed by long term devastation. The man who can add ten people to your church today can be the same one who takes out fifty tomorrow.

Again, our stance isn't anti-church people. I don't believe in looking at every person who comes in from another church as hostile invaders, wolf in sheep's clothing, etc. I don't because I was once such a person. I did not come with an agenda but a desire to live for Jesus. But I also know that not everyone has the same motive. My stance isn't anti-church people but one of responsibility to the people in my church as the shepherd. My responsibility as the shepherd is not to let anyone through the door who would be a potential threat.

So, as much as that rests with us, we need to be patient. We need to wait and assess and let the Lord speak to us as to when is the right time to release such a person into ministry.

# 4. FAITHFULLY YOURS

There were a few more things that could have been listed in regards to the chapter about the six month waiting period for ministry but I believed that they warranted their own section as the information was too much to be contained in just one chapter.

I did mention briefly that one danger in consistently putting people in ministry before the six month period is that it puts the church in a position of being held to ransom by the whims of talented people. New Christians for the most part do not understand the seriousness of ministry and the need for faithfulness. By putting them in ministry too early, it stunts their ability to comprehend this importance. Ministry isn't seen as service but performing or helping out when they feel like. But what happens when they don't feel like helping out?

How many impact teams will be aborted because at the last minute ministers do not feel like helping out? How many church services will be hindered because ministers do not feel a sense of responsibility? How many church plays will be cancelled because ministers do not feel like being dependable?

This may not be seen in catastrophic 'High Definition' in many of our churches but it happens frequently in the church world. I remember once while pioneering in Manchester that a work colleague who happened to be a Christian told me of an embarrassing situation in her church the Sunday before.

She was a very important member of her church's praise and worship team but that Sunday she felt too tired to get up and go to church. She justified it in her mind that the other members of the worship team would cover her and she would go to church that Sunday evening well rested.

She then laughed with slight embarrassment as she told me the rest of the story. It seemed that everyone else on the worship team had the same idea and so no one showed up for church that Sunday morning! I was a new pastor then and that story made me realise the importance of faithfulness. It was then that I was truly impacted on just why we make such a fuss on people being faithful to church.

## FAITHFULNESS MAKES THE WORLD GO ROUND

If you think about it, the whole world runs on faithfulness. We require our buses, trains and planes to run on time. We require our spouses to be devoted. We require, without thought, that our wages be put into our bank account at the end of the month. We require our planes to get us to our determined destination without any hiccups.

So if a plane crashes once every year, if a stove breaks down once a month or if the brakes on a car fail once a week then they cannot be called faithful. If the bank has financial issues every now and again or if a company can't pay wages every six months or so then they can't be called faithful.

Not only are they unfaithful but they also create insecurity. Who would drive a car whose brakes fail once a week? Who would put their faith in a plane that has a history of engine problems? Who would save with a bank that looks like it is about to collapse? No one with a right mind that is.

What if we missed work once a week? Do you think we would last very long in that job? Our unfaithfulness makes us a liability and will hinder the effectiveness of our company.

Faithfulness is what makes the world goes round. It is what makes us save at our banks, what makes us leave one job and take another, what makes us take one flight after another, etc. Without faithfulness this world could come to a complete halt. From the smallest family all the way up to the biggest organisation, for them to be effective everyone needs to be faithful.

If that is true and we know it is true, then it means it is also true for the church. Why is it that people feel somehow that this does not apply to the church? Is the church not important enough for its members to be faithful? Are not the words of Jesus concerning the church true?

If the common bee recognises its need to be faithful to its role in the hive; how much more us? Yet for some of us we don't think so. It's amazing how we take for granted the need of faithfulness to make a major corporation turn around but we feel that we can give unfaithful service to the Church and expect it to have impact.

Some have even looked at the call to faithfulness as a means of dictatorial control! Try telling that to your boss! No one has a problem working 9-5 trying to make a profit for the company they work for but even Christian people have a problem with faithfulness to their ministries so that the Church can have impact in the community.

## FAITHFULNESS AND THE CHURCH

The apostle Paul points out in 1 Corinthians 4:2 that *"...it is required in stewards that one be found faithful."* Faithfulness is of fundamental importance to a minister in the local church. But we don't give out ministry and then tell people to be faithful. We look for people who are already faithful in church knowing that they can be trustworthy with a ministry. If a new convert is looking for ministry we let them know that ministry is only given to someone who will always be faithful. We explain just how unfaithfulness hinders the church and so ministry can't be given to those who will, in effect, let the team down.

So we look for people who already have a good attitude towards faithfulness. Jesus shows us the reality of human nature when He said in Luke 16:10, *"He who is faithful in what is least is faithful also in much..."* If you place an individual in ministry who has a history of being in and out of the church I can guarantee you that he or she will be in and out of ministry.

Six months of being on the sidelines should create in individuals an appreciation for the ministry. I remembered when I came to church and for six months I was watching other people getting involved and I had to sit down. The only thing I could do was help set up the chairs but there were already three ushers for that and there would be times they would say, *"We'll handle that!"* I remembered Pastor Stephens calling a ministry meeting and it burned me that I couldn't be involved because I was not in ministry. So finally, when the time arrived that I could be in ministry, I took it with both hands as to me it was a privilege.

My first ministry was being an usher and I can remember how I'd almost break my neck coming from work to be the first usher at church on a Wednesday evening. I don't think I would have appreciated ministry if I was thrown into it the very first week I came to church.

## THE NECESSITY OF FAITHFULNESS IN THE CHURCH

Another reason why you want people who are faithful is that they are faithful because they love Jesus. They love to be faithful to the things of God and so their motive for faithfulness isn't just so that they have a ministry they are passionate about (which is a good thing) but because of their relationship with God. It means regardless of how they feel, whether they feel lousy about the day or they have the joy of the Lord, nothing will stop them living for Jesus and nothing will stop them from being in the house of the Lord when it is open.

Hebrews 10:25 states *"...not forsaking the assembling of ourselves together, as is the manner of some, but exhorting one another, and so much the more as you see the Day approaching."*

There are two words that stick out in this verse and these are (a) forsaking and (b) assembling. The word 'forsaking' from the original Greek scripture is 'to leave in the lurch, forsake, desert, abandon...'' The word 'assembling' means 'the complete collection'.

Spiros Zodhiates, the author of 'The Complete Wordstudy Dictionary: New Testament', in his translation of the Greek word for 'assembling' states *"Hebrews 10:25* does not merely denote the assembling of corporate worship as a solitary or occasional act, but as customary conduct. The preposition, epi...must refer to Christ Himself as the One to whom this assembly was attached. Thus it would have the meaning of not betraying one's attachment to Jesus Christ and other believers, not avoiding one's own personal responsibility as part of the body of Christ."

In other words, every time there is a church service it is only right for every believer to be there as a part of the collective making the complete collection. It also means that any believer that is not there has in effect forsaken and abandoned the church. It is like the soldier who runs away from the foxhole leaving his friends behind to fight the enemy while he saves his own skin.

This seems very harsh but when you consider the definition of the term 'assembling' as being 'the complete collection' you can understand why. The greatest example of the term 'complete collection' is the alphabet. All twenty six letters are needed to make things happen.

All the books in the English speaking world are down to these twenty six letters. Imagine if one of those letters decided to depart and do his thing and let the other twenty five get on with it. The result would be tragic.

Th_ _ntir_ plan_t would b_ in utt_r b_wild_rm_nt and p_rpl_xity if th_ l_tt_r '_' was _liminat_d from the alphab_t. It'd take ag_s for p_opl_ to disc_rn what was b_ing said. Y_s, w_ could probably g_t along to a d_gr__ but lif_ would b_ a lot _asi_r if th_ l_tt_r that was missing r_turn_d again. Who'd imagin_ that th_ abs_nc_ of on_ littl_ lett_r could caus_ such inconv_ni_nc_. Just lik_ th_ l_tt_r '_' w_ all hav_ our plac_ in the ass_mbly. Unl_ss w_ ar_ th_r_ th_ pow_r of th_ gath_ring is diminish_d.

I bet reading the above paragraph was hard work.

Eventually we were able to get through it in the end but it took far longer than was necessary. All because one member of the alphabet 'forsook' its friends and left them to continue without its help. Faithfulness matters and the tragedy is that it is something we take for granted and only realise the full implication of its importance when people are unfaithful.

## CONTENDING FOR FAITHFULNESS

The reality of life is that things do not always function like clockwork. At the best of times things can go wrong. During a major revival the song leader falls sick or the morning of an impact team the driver of the minibus rings to say that he has to work that Saturday. These things happen but we would be making life worse for ourselves if we allowed unfaithful people to be involved in ministries that would hinder the impact of the church.

The issue of faithfulness is something we have to contend for and something we have to defend. I have had in the past people coming to church who were good people, talented people and people with a righteous testimony but who did not come out to all the services.

As much as I'd like to use them I know that decision would hurt me in the long run. They would be used as an excuse by other people as to why they don't need to be faithful. I would have no authority to pull them up for not being faithful. *"Well Sister Suzy only comes Sunday morning and Wednesday evening service, so why can't I?"* In the end we will find ourselves in a position like so many other churches where you have no idea how each service is going to turn out.

It is because of this dreaded outcome I have to be hard on such people and tell them "No". In most cases I have lost such people to other churches who would cater to their part time involvement. Though it pains me to see them go the future cannot be sacrificed for the present.

Years ago I heard a preacher use the term 'church growth transfer'. Up until that point I never heard of it but it is simply the fact that many churches are seeing growth, not from converts getting saved but people leaving one church and moving on to a next. We can't afford to build a church like that. Our converts must be our own and our ministers not seduced to stay by the 'bait' of ministry. We must take the high road, no matter how difficult it is, that we can see the true foundation created.

## LOVING WHO WE ARE BUT HATING WHAT WE DO

There is a great irony experienced in our churches. Most of our congregation have been saved and brought up in the Potter's House. They have never experienced Christianity in another church. This includes the fact that they have never experienced a church where faithlessness is the norm. They have never been to a church where the song leader leaves after the song service has finished, where the keyboard player is still in bed sleeping or the elder whose job it is to open the church turns up half an hour late.

They would all be appalled to attend such a service yet there are people who feel that our standard in regards to faithfulness is just too much. They don't realise that it is this standard that has made the church what it is and any letting down would make us degenerate into an ineffective church like I mentioned above. Faithfulness adds a professionalism to the church and dare I say it also adds a sense of value, that what we do, is so important that we have no choice but to be faithful to it.

Faithfulness communicates an unconscious

message to the rest of the church and people who attend that our church is important and what we do is vital. This unconscious message attracts people to the church because if we are to attend a church or make a particular church our base, we would rather attend one that is going somewhere rather than one that is going nowhere.

Similarly, faithlessness communicates an unconscious message that these people are not serious, they don't have their act together and they do not value what they do. If they don't value their own church it will only mean that those who visit will not value it either.

# FAITHFULNESS: THE GREAT AID OF PIONEERING

We need to remember that most of us did not start off with hundreds of people in a wonderful church building filled with state of the art equipment. Most of us started off in humble community centres with a couple of Peavey speakers and dodgy mikes. Our praise and worship music came from self-playing keyboards and our song leaders were so out of tune it would make dogs howl.

What made people keep coming back and what caused the church to grow was more than our 'dynamic' preaching. Ultimately, we know it was Jesus but one significant reason that kept people open (so that Christ could draw them) was the unconscious messages given out that in spite of the humble external surroundings we had something going on. There was something important and powerful about what we do. There was something that attracted them to us.

One of these things was our dedication to our vision and our passion for Jesus which was seen in our faithful devotion to the things of God. Week in and week out, whether rain, snow, sleet or sunshine we were at our posts doing what we needed to do with a joy in our hearts and a spring in our steps. Maybe people saw us as nutters at first but after a while they began to see that there had to be something more than that. What they began to see was our faith manifested in our faithfulness.

It is very interesting to note that the New Testament Greek word for 'faith', that is 'pistis', is the same Greek word for 'faithfulness'. In other words, there is no distinction between faith and faithfulness in the word of God. The level of my faith in God is seen by those around me by the level of my faithfulness to the things of God. Thus a church filled with faith is really a church filled with faithfulness and a church filled with faith is only possible if it is a church filled with faithful people.

## 5. SHOW ME AN EXAMPLE

Ideally, exampleship is something that all Christians should observe and practise. After all our Lord Jesus did say in Matthew 5:14-16 that *"You are the light of the world... Let your light so shine before men, that they may see your good works and glorify your Father in heaven."* Our role as Christians in the world is to let people see our righteous character and example, a contrast to the darkness of the world we live in, as it would point people to God.

We have heard so much about being "the light of the world" that it is possible that we just assume that everyone gets the message. It is so taken for granted that many times we fail to realise that this is a critical standard when it comes to being involved in ministry. We must never assume that those who are in ministry will automatically be examples simply because they are in the Potter's House and they have heard a few sermons on being examples.

This subtle standard is something we must come to grips with if we are to have ministers who will help build the church and have impact in the world around us.

There are a number of reasons why exampleship is so important when we are in ministry.

## EXAMPLESHIP IS REFLECTING JESUS

Firstly, exampleship is the by-product of our relationship with God. It is the reflection of our spiritual relationship with Jesus Christ. Though Jesus did say in Matthew 5:14 that we are *"...the light of the world..."* we must also remember that this was only possible because He is *"...the light of the world..."* (John 8:12). If we are this world's light it is only because we are a reflection of Him!

Our character is a result of us wanting to be like Jesus. We want to be righteous because He is righteous. We want to be holy because He is holy. We want to be gentle because He is gentle.

Being a real Christian is more important than being in ministry. It is about being like Him. Before we get into a rush wanting to do something in the church let our first motive be for us to want to be like Jesus. If this is not so, we can become distracted and think exampleship is the rules by which we live in order to be used in the church rather than something we need to be because we have a relationship with Jesus.

The danger of this is we can become two faced hypocrites. That is, we may look the part but it is only surface level because our motive was wrong in the first place.

What we need are people who are examples, not because it is their priority is to be examples, but because they have a real relationship with Jesus Christ that has transformed their lives where they become good examples for the kingdom of God.

Such exampleship is powerful in the church because it is coming from real people. It is coming from people who pray because they want to get closer to God. It is coming from people who read the bible because they want to know how best to live for Jesus. It is coming from people who live right because they want to know how to please the Lord.

## EXAMINED EXAMPLESHIP EXPLAINED

Secondly, being in ministry means we represent Christianity and our church. In a sense we live in a fishbowl and the community in which we live will be watching us very closely to see if we are who we say we are.

The irony is that although the world hates the church judging them they are in effect our fiercest critics. They are watching every move we make and sniffing for any signs of hypocrisy, double standards and unchristian lifestyles.

There are a myriad of motives for this. For one, there are some who are natural cynics who believe that we are 'make believe' and if they just hang around watching us for long enough that after a while they will scratch through the surface and see us for who we truly are – charlatans and frauds.

Then there are those who are truly looking for an answer and are hoping that we are indeed the genuine article who would bring them the solutions they long for.

It would be a real shame that we who represent the church in whatever form act so spiritual in church on Sunday but during the week, the non-Christians who have been watching us see something completely different.

I would compare the gospel to an unmoving nail and our example to a hammer. Just like a hammer gives the nail the force to penetrate wood, our example gives the gospel the power to penetrate the hearts of those around us. There is no point in us sharing the gospel to people if they know that we are not living our lives in agreement with the word of God.

I remember working for a Jamaican finance company in London many years ago. Its purpose was to help Jamaicans living in England who had their savings in bank accounts held Jamaica. This company had a number of agents throughout Britain that helped these account holders do their business.

I remembered one agent was the elder of a particular Jamaican church in London. He was selected because of his reputation as a man of God but to make a long story short he swindled nearly ninety thousand pounds from the company. This further reinforced to my unbelieving General Manager that Christianity was a farce.

It is said that "actions speak louder than words". People would rather see a bible lived out in our lives rather than us reading one to them. The world in general will ignore us but the minute we say we are Christians they will keep that knowledge at the back of their minds and from that day onwards they are watching every move we make.

So our exampleship is important and the people we put in ministry must be a people of example. In a time where so many churches have lost their Christian influence and in a generation where non-Christians are cynical about the Church we can't afford to play games with exampleship.

We can't help people lying about us or slandering

us but we can do our best to make sure that the people who represent us are ones who are shining the light of Christ to the world around us.

## EXAMPLESHIP THE MEANS OF IMITATION

The third reason why exampleship matters is, like I have said before, "actions speak louder than words". Real Christianity is "Do as I do" and not "Do as I say". This is not only because real Christianity is free from hypocrisy but it also is far easier to teach someone by example than it is by speaking.

As a church we need to remember we are reaching sinners and not other Christians. New converts coming into the church are raw and completely ignorant. They are in completely new and unfamiliar surroundings. So in order to fit in they are going to copy what we do. That's human nature. We learn by imitation.

When they see people lifting their hands to worship it is only a matter of time before they too start to lift their hands. They don't know why we lift our hands but they see it and copy. They see us singing the songs and they start to sing as well. They have no idea why they sing but they see it is what we do. But eventually they will get it why we do what we do but for now they imitate.

New Christians learn what it is to be Christians from the older saints. They pray how we pray. They sing the way we sing. They read like we read. They avoid nightclubs like how we avoid nightclubs. They don't smoke because we don't smoke. They don't fool around with the opposite sex like how we don't fool around with the opposite sex.

Our example determines what type of Christian they are going to be. If we are the main people in the church and in the limelight it is our example that they are going to follow. So it would be counterproductive to have someone who is in ministry, singing at a concert or performing at a drama or involved in outreach but you never see them two services in a row. The new convert who looks up to that person is going to copy that person's conduct. It is a guarantee!

This is why the apostle Paul makes it clear in 2 Timothy 2:2 when he says, *"...the things that you have heard from me among many witnesses, commit these to faithful men who will be able to teach others also."* Paul points out that his example, something seen by many witnesses, should be followed by Timothy. Here is a man who is supremely confident in his own exampleship! In return Timothy should show this example in his life to men who would take it up and then teach that to others.

The apostle Paul was a powerful believer that exampleship can be perfectly imitated. He points this out to the church in 1 Corinthians 4:16-17 when he said, *"Therefore I urge you, imitate me. For this reason I have sent Timothy to you, who is my beloved and faithful son in the Lord, who will remind you of my ways in Christ, as I teach everywhere in every church."*

These verses are so powerful! Paul is saying that he wants the Corinthian church to imitate his exampleship and the means by which he will try to accomplish that is by sending Timothy! In other words Timothy was so much like Paul in his exampleship that by sending Timothy it was like Paul himself went.

Years ago I heard a sermon called 'A-Level Christianity' by Rick Godwin. In it he pointed out that he was watching a friend of his who was an excellent pool player. Rick was amazed at this man's ability to knock the balls around the pool table. At one point he exclaimed,

*"You are the best pool player I have ever seen!"* The man replied, *"I'm only a B-level pool player."* Rick retorted, *"What do you mean B-level? I've never seen anyone as good as you!"*

The man explained, *"When I was learning how to play pool I was never exposed to any A-level pool players. Because of that I've picked up the mistakes and practices of B-level players. I'm not good enough to be A-level."*

The point Rick Godwin was making is that we are only as good as the Christians we are around. He added the reason there are so many B-level and C-level Christians around is they got birthed in churches where the Christians who attended them were B-level and C-level.

I believe it was Josh McDowell who stated that the average new Christian is mouldable and pliable in the first two years of their salvation. After that they will be set in their ways.

Once again this shows how important it is that we join our ministries with the right motive. If our motive is for self-glory then ultimately we have no care our example has on the lives of others. If our motive is to help build the church of God then we will realise how counterproductive it is to bring people into the church and then ruin them by our bad example. Thus a right motive into ministry will also motivate us into having a right example.

Exampleship is the reference mark of how the church is to be. It is outline, the framework, and the pattern by which the church is built. We may have different ministries but our exampleship ought to be the same. It is something that must be reinforced time and time again into the lives of new Christians by the consistent lifestyle lived by every minister of the church.

Though I have done my best to present a case for

the importance of exampleship the unfortunate reality is that exampleship is many times undermined by human nature. The manifestation of this human nature is a subconscious disposition to find the path of least resistance, that is, to do as little as possible and get away with it.

## THE PATH OF LEAST RESISTANCE

Thus my fourth reason why exampleship is so important is that there are those out there who are looking for weaknesses in our character and using it to justify themselves. In other words, people subconsciously want to imitate our worst traits as opposed to our best attributes.

When the Samaritans refused to see Jesus, His disciples James and John said in Luke 9:54 *"Lord, do You want us to command fire to come down from heaven and consume them, just as Elijah did?"* Elijah is Israel's greatest prophet besides Moses. Here is a man who fasted for forty days, who stood up to the tyranny of King Ahab, who faced the prophets of Baal head on and who brought the rains back to Israel.

But which characteristic of Elijah did they remember? They remembered that he called fire from heaven to kill the soldiers of Ahab who disrespected him. John and James are saying that Jesus should emulate that particular response of the great prophet. I have not read of anything where John and James encouraged Jesus to follow the better examples of Elijah.

Human nature seeks out the worst characteristics of those around us to follow rather than their better qualities. As a pastor I have seen this on a number of occasions.

I love books. I have been reading as far back as I

can remember. One of my greatest joys is going through a good book. To say I love book stores is an understatement. I could lie on their floors for hours. Thus the most meaningful present I could give to an individual is a book because it is coming from my heart.

It also means that I get angry with those who abuse books and I find it hard to forgive anyone who mistreats the books I gave them.

I remember once going to a friend's house and to my shock his wife was standing on a one volume Matthew Henry bible commentary I had given him. Why? She was painting the ceiling. In my heart I vowed never to buy him a book ever again.

I have said all that just to make my point on how I love books. But I also have another love. I love comics. To you mockers out there comics were indeed kid stuff back in the 1980s but somehow in the last few years comics have grown up with the readers of that generation. In other words, it is not really kid stuff anymore.

In the pressure of ministry I find it an escape to delve into an issue of the Batman or Green Lantern. So you won't find me only on the floors of Waterstones, Borders or Wesley Owen. You will also find me in the corridors of the 'Forbidden Planet' or 'Another World' as I go through the latest issues of the Justice League and Spiderman.

But I found out something horrific in my early days pastoring the church in Wolverhampton. Though the disciples in my church knew I was an avid reader. Though they have been to my house and seen the books stocked upon books. Instead of reading the books I was reading and talking about the books I was talking about they were reading the comics I was reading and talking about the comics I was talking about!

These guys completely ignored the books and became fixated on the comics. I could understand that if I was only a comic book kind of a guy but I was more into books than comics yet these disciples preferred comics to books! As a result I had to stop buying comics!

The good news is that the craze in comics died after a few months but they never developed that kind of craze in books much to my chagrin.

Why was this? It is far easier to read a comic than it is to read a book. A book may have well over a hundred pages while a comic may have only thirty. A book may have only words while comics have pictures in them. My disciples were not wicked and evil. They just manifested the part of human nature where we take the path of least resistance.

This is why we are to take our example very seriously because wittingly or unwittingly there are people who are going to imitate our worst possible traits.

This doesn't mean we put on ourselves the burden to be perfect. No one can stand up to that kind of pressure. But it does mean we guard our testimony to the best of our abilities.

## EXAMPLESHIP AND LIBERTY

It also means, fifthly, that exampleship demands far more of us than the Bible. This is where the danger of legalism can appear if we misunderstand the motive behind exampleship. This is where we are seen as extremists by other people, even Christians, who fail to see our responsibility to being an example to others.

The apostle Paul clearly stated in 1 Corinthians 8:13, *"Therefore, if food makes my brother stumble, I will never again eat meat, lest I make my brother stumble."*

In context Paul is speaking about foods sacrificed to idols. He points out that an idol is nothing and so eating food sacrificed to idols is not a big deal.

But for some an idol is a big deal and eating foods to idols is an even bigger deal. Though it may be nothing for him to eat food sacrificed to idols it may be something for someone else and if he tries to imitate him without having that confidence he sins against his conscience because whatever is not of faith is sin (Romans 14:23).

So for the sake of brothers like this Paul says that he will not eat meat because his freedom to eat whatever he likes may cause them to stumble into sin.

Reading an issue of the Batman may not be sin but if it affects the discipleship process of the young men in the church, for the sake of exampleship I have to give it up.

There are times when certain things that are not sinful have to be sacrificed in order to help the church keep her effective edge. I believe this is what Jesus meant when He said in John 17:19, *"...for their sakes I sanctify Myself..."*

Though what we do may not be sinful in the eyes of God, so that we don't become a stumbling block to others we guard our testimony and put greater restrictions on ourselves.

There may be some who would like me to list these restrictions but like I said before Christianity isn't rules and regulations but a relationship with Christ. If we have a relationship with Jesus the way the apostle Paul did, He will speak to us and show us the areas in our lives where we may have to go out further on a limb to be examples above reproach.

I could right down a few safe restrictions but what about those that aren't on the list. Will you choose the path of least resistance and say, *"Well, it wasn't in the book so therefore I don't have to do it"*?

Let us go back to the very first reason for exampleship and that is to have a growing relationship with God and to be more like Jesus Christ. If we make it our hearts desire to TRULY be like Christ I believe that we will be the examples our churches need us to be.

# 6. LOOSE CANNONS AND TICKING TIME BOMBS

Another subtle standard that needs to be addressed is the issue of accountability. Accountability is simply the ability to be accountable for what you have done. The fact that it is ability is to be noted as we live in an age of account-dis-ability.

In people's personal lives it is almost an alien concept to have those in your life that you are actually answerable to. Children today are brought up with this mindset that they can do whatever they please without being scrutinised. The very act of scrutiny is an invasion of privacy and a breach of their human rights.

This way of thinking has permeated its way through today's culture. Today's generation can't be tested and confronted by those who know better. The elderly have done so only to experience a few choice expletives words from youngsters who have embraced their 'disability' from the "I don't care" antics of their favourite movie-stars and pop-stars.

We live in an age where accountability in many frameworks is something that we are just not into. We don't like people intruding in our personal lives or trying to restrict our freedoms. Not just that but in our generation there is a very smug self-righteousness in leaving people to do their own thing.

That somehow in leaving people to do whatever they want is us showing how tolerant and open minded we are. Oh, how different we are to those busybodies meddling in people's lives. The reality is many fail to differentiate the difference between control and concern.

In saying that accountability can be abused and right off the bat I'd like to point out that abusing accountability is just as bad as being unaccountable.

We live in a generation where the main sphere of social accountability, between one's family and community, has less significance than years gone by. There was a time where the words of the elders were final and one simply had to submit to them whether you liked them or not. Listening to the advice of one's parents was compulsory. You had to give an account of your education, your career choice and even your choice of a spouse.

My father often told me that when he was growing up that if he was found misbehaving on the road somewhere the unwritten rule was that the neighbours had a right to discipline you right then and there. And after you were given a swift beating you would be reported to your parents who would double the punishment. And woe unto you if you disrespected the school teacher or failed to complete your homework as the cane would come your way and your parents would be notified.

Here is a scary scripture! Deuteronomy 21:18-21 states, *"If a man has a stubborn and rebellious son who will not obey the voice of his father or the voice of his mother, and who, when they have chastened him, will not heed them,* **19** *then his father and his mother shall take hold of him and bring him out to the elders of his city, to the gate of his city.* **20** *And they shall say to the elders of his city, 'This son of ours is stubborn and rebellious; he will not obey our voice; he is a glutton and a drunkard.'* **21** *Then all the men of his city shall stone him to death with stones; so you shall put away the evil from among you, and all Israel shall hear and fear."*

But in society today, the fabric of this form of social accountability is falling apart. Rebellious teenagers are the norm today. Many older people live in fear of being harassed by young adults fuelled by cheap alcohol and drugs. Misdemeanours are committed in broad daylight in the sight of the community yet no one dares to reprimand those responsible for wrong doing for fear of being targeted. Teachers today are not only treated disrespectfully by students but by the parents as well.

There is much to be appreciated in the social framework of the past that can still be seen in Asian and African communities. Their children are generally more respectful and well behaved. The elders are treated with dignity and reverence. Criminality and promiscuity are lower and frowned upon and the children do much better in school.

That's the great work of accountability yet in saying that it is in these same communities that we also hear of horrific abuses. Now and again we read of honour killings where the men in the family will kill a young female for 'dishonouring' her family which simply means she has fallen in love with a young man the family doesn't approve of. Young adults and even teenagers are forced to marry someone against their own will. Children are forced into a career not of their choosing just to please their parents. Conversion to another religion or marrying outside of their race can lead to being cut off from the family and even spat on in the street by relatives and people from the community.

I remember having a Christian family from India come to my church in Wolverhampton a few years ago. A niece of the mother was also living with them. One day the niece came to me informing me that she was moving to London because she could no longer live with her aunt as she was making her life extremely miserable. The niece was twenty-five years old but her aunt insisted that she be at home at 7pm at the latest! Now I do understand that the niece lives in the aunt's house and therefore is subject to her aunt but a 7pm curfew on a twenty-five year old is a bit too much for me.

This book is all about the spirit of the standards. It is not just all about doing the right things but doing the right things in a right way. This is also true with accountability. Though we must expect those who are a part of church ministry to be accountable, steps must also be taken so that accountability is not abused.

As a pastor, we can become so used to people being accountable to us that we can cross the lines without realising it. We can expect and demand things off people we have no right to. I understand the office of a pastor is to be respected but let us not get to the point where we treat grown people as if they were children or talk to erring disciples as if they were naughty schoolboys. Their submission to us is not for our benefit but to further their relationship with God.

I love the story of David while at battle against his

enemies wishing for water from his hometown of Bethlehem. 2 Samuel 23:15-17 reveals that *"***15**...*David said with longing, "Oh, that someone would give me a drink of the water from the well of Bethlehem, which is by the gate!"* **16** *So the three mighty men broke through the camp of the Philistines, drew water from the well of Bethlehem that was by the gate, and took it and brought it to David. Nevertheless he would not drink it, but poured it out to the Lord.* **17** *And he said, "Far be it from me, O Lord, that I should do this! Is this not the blood of the men who went in jeopardy of their lives?" Therefore he would not drink it."*

We must learn the balance of accountability as pastors over a congregation of willing ministers of not taking what belongs to the Lord. It is one thing writing this book to draw attention to my expectations of ministers in the church but with a topic like accountability it is only right for ministers to also have an expectation of me that I would not abuse their trust in me as their pastor. It does go both ways.

It also means that I am accountable to the church for how I live my life.

## ACCOUNTABILITY: THE MEANS OF RIGHT LIVING

Yet accountability is the very means by which this world performs and ticks over. The very reason people have public weddings is to make themselves accountable before man and God that they have taken on very serious vows.

Businesses do their yearly accounts and have their books audited in order to present to the world that they are accountable to the powers that be. In doing this they are declaring to the world that they are trustworthy and have nothing to cover up and hide.

The work environment is where we can't just do our own thing with our time and energy but we must give an account of what we are doing if we are to keep our jobs and keep getting a salary.

But the very fact that there is accountability at work shows that there is a reason behind it. Imagine if no one was accountable at the work place? Imagine the chaos and anarchy that would manifest itself. People would be turning up at all manner of times if they did bother to turn up at all. Phones would not be answered, customer service would be thrown out the window, invoices would not be paid, etc. The list would be endless.

At the end of the day, without accountability, the entire work place would be rendered completely useless and ineffective. The same is true with life outside of accountability.

Whether we like it or not, it doesn't matter who we are, we need to be accountable to someone. We need someone in our lives who is able to ask the hard, difficult and awkward questions we would rather not hear.

We need people poking around in our lives looking for things that are there yet should not be there. We need those people that after fighting and evading their probing questions that we can surrender to and confess the issues that we have been struggling with.

Perhaps this is why James 5:16 says, *"Confess your trespasses to one another, and pray for one another, that you may be healed."* As we can see, healing comes after accountability.

No matter how spiritual we are we need to remember that we are all flawed creatures. Though as Christians we try to live by the power of the Spirit, in all honesty, there are times when the old man, the Adamic sinful nature, manifests itself. For some, this sinfulness is something they are powerless to deal with and for others it is something they are unaware of.

Accountability helps us to deal with those issues before they become bigger or more dangerous. It helps to minimise the potential damage and fall out of a life going out of control.

It short, accountability keeps you in check; it keeps you from being too big for your boots.

## LOOSE CANNONS

In life there are such things as loose cannons. The original etymology of the word speaks of cannons not tied down in a ship and so during a ferocious storm with the winds and waves battering the ship, these cannons are loose, moving to and fro smashing into things and creating all kinds of havoc inside the ship.

Without accountability, being kept in check, every individual has the ability to be a loose cannon creating all kinds of trouble for themselves and others.

This is very true in the church. The last thing any church needs is a member who is unaccountable, a loose cannon creating more trouble for the church than benefits.

Ministry without accountability is like handing matches to a five year old. You don't put something that powerful into the hands of someone who has no sense of responsibility. This ultimately works out to bring grief and setback to the local church.

Ministry is responsibility. When an individual is given ministry that person in a sense has been given authority and freedom of expression in the church.

Someone in ministry is seen as sanctioned by the church, who has credibility and 'weight' in the congregation. In other words, such a person is seen as influential.

In any organisation it is desired that influential people are those who are working for the good of that establishment. That such people are aware of their influence and use it to build up and not to tear down. In other words such people of influence are responsible in how they conduct themselves. They don't do whatever whim that comes to mind but they think about how their behaviour will affect that institution.

A good example of a loose cannon is King Uzziah. Uzziah was a good man when he became king of Israel. However, as the expression goes, *"Absolute power corrupts absolutely"*.

In 2 Chronicles 26:16-21 we read of King Uzziah. *"***16** *But when he was strong his heart was lifted up, to his destruction, for he transgressed against the Lord his God by entering the temple of the Lord to burn incense on the altar of incense.* **17** *So Azariah the priest went in after him, and with him were eighty priests of the Lord – valiant men.* **18** *And they withstood King Uzziah, and said to him, "It is not for you, Uzziah, to burn incense to the Lord, but for the priests, the sons of Aaron, who are consecrated to burn incense. Get out of the sanctuary, for you have trespassed! You shall have no honor from the Lord God."* **19** *Then Uzziah became furious; and he had a censer in his hand to burn incense. And while he was angry with the priests, leprosy broke out on his forehead, before the priests in the house of the Lord, beside the incense altar.* **20** *And Azariah the chief priest and all the priests looked at him, and there, on his forehead, he was leprous; so they thrust him out of that place. Indeed he also hurried to get out, because the Lord had struck him.* **21** *King Uzziah was a leper until the day of his death. He dwelt in an isolated house, because he was a leper; for he was cut off from the house of the Lord."*

Uzziah became too big for his boots. He thought that because he was the king of Judah that he could do whatever he wanted. As king, he felt he was not accountable to anyone. No one could tell him what to do even when he was confronted by the high priest and eighty other priests. He felt he could go beyond the boundaries that were placed around him.

He did not regard the fact that he was of the tribe of Judah and as a result had no business doing the priestly work which was reserved for the tribe of Levi alone. As a result God judged him with a skin condition that barred him from the house of God.

Another king who started out good was Joash who was initially accountable to his uncle Jehoiada when he became king. 2 Chronicles 24:2 states, *"Joash did what was right in the sight of the Lord all the days of Jehoiada the priest."*

But when Jehoiada died Joash span out of control and began to do his own thing and worship idols.

God sent a prophet, Zechariah the son of Jehoiada, a first cousin to the king to talk him out of his madness but Joash not only refused to listen but also had his own flesh and blood murdered.

2 Chronicles 24:20-22 states, *"**20** Then the Spirit of God came upon Zechariah the son of Jehoiada the priest, who stood above the people, and said to them, "Thus says God:'Why do you transgress the commandments of the Lord, so that you cannot prosper? Because you have forsaken the Lord, He also has forsaken you.'" **21** So they conspired against him, and at the command of the king they stoned him with stones in the court of the house of the Lord. **22** Thus Joash the king did not remember the kindness which Jehoiada his father had done to him, but killed his son; and as he died, he said, "The Lord look on it, and repay!""*

What we can learn as well is that even the best of people can become corrupted and that is why every one of us, without exception, need to be accountable to someone so that the good can remain good.

King David is one of the greatest examples of a good king left to himself and not being held accountable as king.

David, as spiritual as he was, became too big for his boots. His big mistake was seducing a beautiful married woman, murdering her husband and marrying her to obscure the fact that he had got her pregnant during the affair.

The sad thing is that David did not know how far he had gone in his corruption. God had to bring David in check by sending the prophet Nathan his way.

In 2 Samuel 12:7-13 we read, *"7Then Nathan said to David, "You are the man! Thus says the Lord God of Israel: 'I anointed you king over Israel, and I delivered you from the hand of Saul. 8I gave you your master's house and your master's wives into your keeping, and gave you the house of Israel and Judah. And if that had been too little, I also would have given you much more! 9Why have you despised the commandment of the Lord, to do evil in His sight? You have killed Uriah the Hittite with the sword; you have taken his wife to be your wife, and have killed him with the sword of the people of Ammon. 10Now therefore, the sword shall never depart from your house, because you have despised Me...13So David said to Nathan, "I have sinned against the Lord.""*

It was only then that David realised just how far he had gone and he repented and got his heart right.

Unfortunately, although he was restored in his relationship with God, he had gone too far and had now gave the God he served and his faith a bad name.

2 Samuel 12:13-14 states, *"Nathan said to David, "The Lord also has put away your sin; you shall not die. However, because by this deed you have given great occasion to the enemies of the Lord to blaspheme..."*

## WE ARE ANSWERABLE TO A HIGHER POWER

Right here we understand one of the most fundamental principles of accountability. As ministers in the church we are not to be doing our own thing but God's things. We need to remember we are working for God and not for ourselves and when we forget that important truth we are only bringing harm our way.

Jesus made this clear in a parable He spoke to His disciples in Luke 16:1-2 saying, *"There was a certain rich man who had a steward, and an accusation was brought to him that this man was wasting his goods. So he called him and said to him, 'What is this I hear about you? Give an account of your stewardship..."*

The steward or manager is not the owner but acts on behalf of the owner and as manager he has to give an account of his activities. By giving account we are acknowledging that there is someone higher over us and ultimately this person is God Himself.

Whether this world recognises it or not the reality is that every single man or woman in this world is accountable to God who will ultimately one day hold them in account. Romans 14:10-12 makes it fearfully plain that *"...we shall all stand before the judgment seat of Christ. For it is written: "As I live, says the Lord, every knee shall bow to Me, and every tongue shall confess to God." So then each of us shall give account of himself to God."*

Unfortunately many people feel it is all about them when it is all about Jesus. And there are times when people don't realise that it is all about then and nothing to do with Jesus. And then there are times when people have forgotten that it is all about Jesus and made themselves the focus.

What we can learn from Uzziah and David is that even good people in church can be carried away by their own talents and their ministries. Without accountability not only are we doing our own thing but many times we are running contrary with what God is doing. We are loose cannons and time bombs waiting to explode and when we do it is the name of Jesus and the reputation of the church that gets hurt.

There are those who feel the purpose of accountability is to control people. Far from it! Accountability is to make sure that everyone stays in the flow of the Spirit and in the vision of the Church.

## HAVING HARMONY WHILE SEEKING IMPACT

The purpose of accountability is harmony. Consider an orchestra. Every member of that orchestra has a certain role and function in which to play. Not one of them has the liberty to do their own thing as that would hinder the flow and harmony of the orchestra.

Every one of those instruments are submitted and accountable to the conductor who directs each instrument, not for his own glory, but for the harmony and effectiveness of the entire orchestra. Without this accountability, the orchestra would be sheer noise as each instrument seeks its own glory but with accountability there is harmony and joy.

All it takes is one maverick violinist or trombonist to wreck the harmony of the entire orchestra. It is that simple! The conductor is no means an ogre or dictator but someone who sees and understands the bigger picture.

This is the same idea behind the church. All it takes is for one loose cannon to disrupt the harmony of the congregation. That is just how fragile the harmony of an orchestra is. That isn't an over-exaggeration. I have seen loose cannons in action and it is anything but harmonious. Ecclesiastes 9:18 points out that *"...one sinner destroys much good."*

I can recall going on an international impact team years ago. Looking back I don't think there were more than a dozen of us. Bear in mind that an international impact team is not a standard impact team. In a standard impact team there is usually a diverse set of individuals you can choose from to send to another city. (We know when you are pioneering you send what you have!) But in an international impact team those who are there are a result of those who are able to pay for their trip. That makes a whole world of difference.

I have found that over the years that a good portion of those on an international impact team were never a part of the concert scene back in their home church. But in order to make the international team have impact it is every hand on deck and it is wonderful to see creativity spring out of urgency and limitation.

I have seen those who have never performed back home rapping and singing on the streets and performing in concerts. Those without an ounce of singing ability are not hindered either as they perform a drama or a skit. Who would have thought they could act with such passion and sincerity?

It could have been a completely joyous and harmonious affair if it wasn't for one individual who just wouldn't get with the programme. With only a handful of performers he wouldn't rap because he has an itch in his throat.

Come on! We have travelled thousands of miles to get here and you won't perform? It's not like we are back home and we have others in church we can call upon to take your place! Can't you sacrifice? Can't you just rise above it?

This happens in churches world over. He wouldn't rap because he has been in the sun for too long during the day and he is tired. She wouldn't perform in the skit because she didn't get the part she wanted. He wouldn't do the altar call because he wasn't given enough notice.

This is a great example of unfaithfulness as faithfulness is the ability to be dependable regardless of the situation. A worker who has never skipped work in forty years had to be flexible in various situations in order to have been faithful. He may have had issues with sickness or traffic or wintry conditions but he was always able to find a way to work.

The reason, however, why I have included this in the accountability section as opposed to faithfulness is that in this case we see people who are unwilling to listen. They have their own agenda that they exalt ahead of the agenda of Christ. Their feelings or their rest is far more important than doing something for the kingdom of God. And they have no intention of listening or obeying those who are in charge.

They put a dampener on the whole team because

the other members are just as tired as they are. They too have been in the hot sun. They too may be feeling the effects of jet lag. But they are willing to put aside all that for the purpose of why they were there in the first place and that is to reach people for Jesus. They don't find it fair that one person should have the power to shipwreck all that they were trying to do.

Accountability is recognising that I have a responsibility to others. It means I just can't do my own thing at the expense of others. It means I'm not free to do whatever I want because what I do affect others either or good or for bad.

Being accountable makes life easy on everyone and really it is not too much to ask. No one is asking for slavish devotion. What we are all looking for is smooth and harmonious progress for the church and accountability helps in achieving that.

Accountability in church is quite simple.

It is making a phone call to your ministry's leader to let them know you won't make it because you are sick or at work or whatever.

It is having a humble disposition and making yourself open to receive instruction or correction without being contentious and making life difficult for the instructor.

It is recognising you are a part of a team and that you have a responsibility to them.

Accountability is not only to the pastor of the church. We live in such a rebellious age. There are those who after years will listen to the pastor but not to anyone else. Accountability is not only submitting to the pastor but to anyone who is over you. Make life harmonious by listening to the concert director, drama team leader, the rap/music group leader, usher or anyone else in some kind of authority. Make their lives and their ministries easier for them.

## BEING ACCOUNTABLE IS LOOKING OUT FOR OUR BEST INTEREST

But accountability doesn't only help the church; it also helps the individual as well.

We are all fallen creatures and the best of us have limited insight into everything. At times we need people to help us to see things that by ourselves we would not be able to see. Even the wisest of individuals have blind spots and without the aid of others we'd find ourselves in a pit unable to climb out.

Proverbs 11:14 points out that *"where there is no counsel, the people fall; but in the multitude of counsellors there is safety."* Giving people access into our lives is a great help in keeping us making right decisions and staying blessed.

Find someone who is unaccountable and you will find someone who will eventually self destruct.

Mike Tyson is considered one of the greatest fighters ever to have put on a boxing glove. Throughout his entire teenage years he was under the tutelage of the famous old trainer Cus D'Amato. When D'Amato died Mike was coached by Cus' disciple Kevin Rooney who led Mike Tyson to become the youngest heavyweight champion of all time.

Eventually Mike believed his own hype and fired Rooney and hired his friends to 'coach' him. The reality is that he felt he was his own man and didn't need anyone to help him. He was unaccountable to anyone because in his own words he was 'the baddest man on the planet'.

Well, the world's baddest man faced an unknown James 'Buster' Douglas who beat Mike silly. During the middle rounds when Mike was being beaten up and did not know what to do his friends stood there helpless unable to help because they were not coaches. So, being unaccountable does have its drawbacks.

Life functions in such a way that individuals by themselves will not be able to make it all of the way. We all need people in our lives who will help us go further and that is only possible when we make ourselves accountable to them.

# 7. TITHING ME CRAZY

Generally, when it comes to an exposition on tithing the usual line of argument is to speak about the personal benefits. Most of the sermons you hear and books you will read about tithing speak of the blessing that comes your way if you do tithe. So, if you are in church long enough, you get to understand why tithing is beneficial to you and a lack of tithing is to your disadvantage.

In this book, however, we will speak of the need for tithing from a completely different angle. This rarely spoken of point deals with our personal responsibility to the upkeep of the church of God as an important part in the ministerial standards we have as a fellowship.

This is where the rubber meets the road as giving to receive is a great incentive to tithe but giving because it is our duty to is not. Not only is giving because it is our duty not an incentive, to the natural man it is completely unreasonable. After all, who in their right mind pays a company to work for the same? The normal course of events is that we are paid to do a job. Yet in the church we are told we have to give in order to qualify to be used in the church.

What a rip off!

Or is it?

## THE BLESSING OF TITHING

Before we get into the nitty-gritty of our personal responsibility of tithing I want to briefly look at the blessing of tithing.

Perhaps the most well known bible verses that speak of the advantages of tithing and disadvantages of not tithing is found in the book of Malachi.

Malachi 3:8-12 states, *"**8** "Will a man rob God? Yet you have robbed Me! But you say, 'In what way have we robbed You?' In tithes and offerings. **9** You are cursed with a curse, for you have robbed Me, even this whole nation. **10** Bring all the tithes into the storehouse, that there may be food in My house, and try Me now in this," says the Lord of hosts, "If I will not open for you the windows of heaven and pour out for you such blessing that there will not be room enough to receive it. **11** "And I will rebuke the devourer for your sakes, so that he will not destroy the fruit of your ground, nor shall the vine fail to bear fruit for you in the field," says the Lord of hosts; **12** And all nations will call you blessed, for you will be a delightful land," says the Lord of hosts."*

From these verses we get to understand a few things. Firstly, the tithe belongs to God. Leviticus 27:30 confirms this by saying, *"...the tithe...is the Lord's. It is holy to the Lord."* This means that although we may be in possession of things, the initial ten percent of what we have plus freewill offerings belong to God. That means if we fail to give them up it means we have robbed God because He is the rightful proprietor, not us.

Secondly, by not tithing, that is, by robbing God we are automatically cursed by God in the area of our finances. Supernaturally we are affected by "the devourer". In other words, in the supernatural realm forces are at work attacking our finances making our money not go as much as we would have liked or calculated.

Thirdly, by giving God what is His He blesses what we have left and makes our 90% or less more than 100%. He makes sure that what we have is prosperous and this blessing will be evident to all those around us.

## MAINTAINING THE PHYSICAL SIDE OF THE CHURCH

But this book is not about the blessing of tithing but its purpose in our standards. In other words, it is not about the benefits of tithing but rather, the responsibilities of tithing.

Tithing is the means by which the work of God is supported. You remove the framework of tithing from the church and you remove the means by which the church is able to have impact in the community and the world. The Church may be spiritual bride of Christ and supernatural in origin but it has a physical and dare I say a financial part as well.

In other words, although the church is about prayer, evangelism, the move of the Holy Spirit, deliverance, salvation and all these spiritual terms it is also about buying flyers to advertise services, concerts, revivals and dramas. It is about paying rent on community centres for various outreach activities. It is about paying the lease or mortgage on a church building. It is about paying for the gas, electric and water. As a matter of fact, a significant portion of the church activities is about paying. Fullstop!

Without tithing everything comes to a standstill no matter how spiritual the activity may be. Nehemiah 13:10-12 says, *"I also realized that the portions for the Levites had not been given them; for each of the Levites and the singers who did the work had gone back to his field. So I contended with the rulers, and said, "Why is the house of God forsaken?" And I gathered them together and set them in their place. Then all Judah brought the tithe of the grain and the new wine and the oil to the storehouse."*

The Levites were men who were willing to do God's work but they had families to feed and as a result the house of God was forsaken. As excitable and enthusiastic as Nehemiah was he realised that the revival of their faith was not going to happen until the Levites were able to solely focus on the ministry as opposed to their daily bread. Tithing made that possible.

Many people fail to see or underestimate the financial cost in running a church and keeping the church afloat every month. It is because of this – ignorance – why people who are not committed to tithing and giving say silly things like *"Why don't we believe God that the landlord will give us the building rent free?"* or *"Let's pray that the reading on the electric metre moves slowly so we can get cheap electric every month."* Or the cheapskates complain, *"Why do we have to use glossy fliers? Why can't we just draw something using ClipArt and get it photocopied at someone's workplace for free?"*

These may seem like spiritual people with great faith or shrewd financial savvy but in reality these are people who have no intent to obey the scriptures in regards to tithing and giving. Their money is very much their own and they intend to keep it that way. If they had a company ask them if they'd use ClipArt for their artwork. Why don't they believe God that their mortgage would be free for a year?

The reason they will be 'spiritual' for the church and 'unspiritual' for them is because their faith is superficial. The reason their faith is superficial is because the church is not that significant to them.

Okay, let us believe God that we won't have to pay rent for a year. If 'somehow' God doesn't move for us and we are evicted to them it is *"Oh, well! Let us hope we get another building."* But do you think they would say the same thing or act the same way if they were about to lose their house? As a matter of fact, they wouldn't wait for God to bring deliverance. They would be working every hour God sent in order to make sure every payment was made.

The church doesn't need the 'faith' of self-absorbed Christians who have no concern but for their own things. It doesn't need the hollow 'prayers' spoken by people who wouldn't believe God if those prayers were for themselves.

## ARGUING OUR WAY OUT OF RESPONSIBILITY FOR THE CHURCH

It needs men and women of responsibility who take the house of God as seriously as their own houses. This isn't a Potter's House rule but God's rule.

Haggai 1:3-9 points out that *"...the word of the Lord came by Haggai the prophet, saying,* **4** *"Is it time for you yourselves to dwell in your paneled houses, and this temple to lie in ruins?"* **5** *Now therefore, thus says the Lord of hosts: "Consider your ways!* **6** *"You have sown much, and bring in little; you eat, but do not have enough; you drink, but you are not filled with drink; you clothe yourselves, but no one is warm; and he who earns wages, earns wages to put into a bag with holes."* **7** *Thus says the Lord of hosts: "Consider your ways!* **8**

*Go up to the mountains and bring wood and build the temple, that I may take pleasure in it and be glorified," says the Lord.* **9** *"You looked for much, but indeed it came to little; and when you brought it home, I blew it away. Why?" says the Lord of hosts. "Because of My house that is in ruins, while every one of you runs to his own house."*

God was never against them living in panelled houses. But here we see a people who thought it perfectly okay to make their lifestyles a priority and completely ignore the things of God. God was against their selfishness where they made sure every detail of their homes was carefully looked after while the house of the Lord was left to rot without so much of an afterthought. That was the killer.

The Bible calls God the just Judge (Psalms 7:11). That means the punishment the Israelites received fitted the crime. And if that is true then it means that the Israelites failure to take personal responsibility for the house of God brought severe losses their way. It shows how serious God views His people taking personal responsibility of the welfare of His house.

This responsibility isn't some half-hearted sense of obligation but God expects us to treat His house the way we would treat our own! Anything less is worthy of judgment.

I mention anything less because you have those who know that they have a personal responsibility to the house of God but the question in their minds is "How much?" The issue is how little can they give and view it as fulfilling their personal responsibility to the house of God.

These are people who will bring a box of Tetley tea to church to help out with the teas and coffees after service or a bag of pencils for the kids in Sunday school. They do this because they see a 'need' and they only want to help. Well, if you tithe then we'd have more than enough tea and pencils for church. The reality is that many 'needs' in the church would be instantly done away with if another two or three people in the church started to tithe.

Then you have those who know that there are financial burdens on the church and know that they need to give but they still won't tithe. Once again it is an amazing thing how people can throw off personal responsibility in a 'spiritual' manner. I have met such people who believe the reason there are needs in the church is that the pastor is not a man of faith.

There was one occasion in Manchester where a couple who visited for a few weeks tried to vilify me for working a job and claiming to be a man of God. According to them, a man of God lives by faith and so doesn't need to work in order to have his needs met. If I was a man of God then every financial need in the church would be met through my faith.

It is easy to say all that when you're not the one responsible for paying the bills. Why should the pastor be the only one with the faith to believe God? Why should the pastor be the only one negotiating with the landlord in regards to rent? Where is the collective personal responsibility?

## BENEFITS WITHOUT RESPONSIBILITIES

Non-tithers want the benefits of church without the cost or sense of responsibility. Somehow, because salvation, forgiveness and prayer are free then coming to a church ought to be free as well.

Again, what's so special about the church? The praise and worship team are not as talented as Rihanna or

Beyonce. The preaching isn't as good as TD Jakes. I have nice friendly chats with people in the church but I can have those same chats down at the local park for free. What exactly is it that I'm paying for?

To these people, the church really has no real value.

There is a real difference between the words – *"This is my church"* and *"This church is the church that I go to"*.

There is the old story of a boy who went to church with his dad. When the offering basket went around his father put in a pound. After the service he said to his dad, *"Not a bad show for a pound."*

People have no problem paying seventy five pounds to go and watch a football match or one hundred pounds to watch Beyonce at the NEC but to pay for church? The question is what do people really think of the church in general? There is a subconscious attitude that people have that causes them not to be givers.

Is it that many churches are in a state of decay? Seemingly chaotic and unprofessional? Lack impressiveness? Rubbish preaching? No vision?

Somehow for some, the church is like social services. They are supposed to get something out of it. Nursery for their kids, encouragement, money to help them pay their gas or electric, etc. But do they ever consider where the resources come from? Why is it okay for some people to be doing all the giving and it is fine for others not to?

## TIED INTO YOUR INVESTMENT

Well, enough of my rants! Maybe there are people who are thinking, what does this have to do with ministry standards? Much in every way! The Lord Jesus said in

Luke 12:34, *"For where your treasure is, there your heart will be also."* Your heart is connected to what you give to. The man who spends £20,000 on a car values it more than a man who got it for free.

This is the same reason why a community in which people who have bought their own houses is in better shape than a community that are all rental properties belonging to the council. Those that have bought their house value it and as a result of that, maintain their houses far better than those who get their rent paid by housing benefit.

When I lived in Manchester years ago, there was an area called Hulme that consisted mainly of council estates where the majority of the people were unemployed and collecting housing benefits. This area was almost completely knocked down and brand new homes and apartment blocks were built (I called it Legoland because it seemed these homes and apartments were made out of multicoloured bricks).

It was interesting that after a few years, when going door to door outreaching in these neighbourhoods that garbage, graffiti, bashed in doors and broken windows were becoming more common in an area that was more or less brand new. Why? They were not valued because the people in them did not give towards their homes.

It is truthful to say that people value what they invest in. But what if by some small chance you found people who did not care in what they invested in. What if a few people in a community where everyone had bought their house began to bash theirs in? Well, the other neighbours, seeing that the property value would go down would do their best to make sure such antisocial behaviour comes to an end. But in a community where the houses are not brought most neighbours won't really care. Refuse can invade the street, broken windows, doors without handles, etc.

So why is tithing mandatory for ministry? Because people who tithe are people who are committed to the church. There are much greater odds that someone who contributes financially to the church will stick around through trials and difficulties than the one who has never given. Giving ties those that give to the thing that they have given to.

We see this all through life. A man falls in love with a young lady and all of a sudden he spends money on extra phone bills, flowers, taking her out, etc. He spends money he would never dream of spends on himself. Why? It is because of love; his heart is into it. And as he spends he is in a sense 'investing' in that relationship which further ties him to it. We all know that the man who has the means but will not spend the money is not all that into her.

I have found it very interesting when the church has gone through seasons where as many as fifteen people have left church in a short space of time yet the total giving from month to month did not change one bit. Why? It could be that those who remained gave more than normal or it could be, and this is more likely, that those who left never gave in the first place.

Being in the ministry for over thirteen years I have seen this to be true. People who never cultivated a habit of regular tithing never usually stay in the church.

To sum things up, the reason those in ministry are required to give is that by their giving they are helping the church to continue and they have made the church their own. If you give someone ministry who has no intention to see the church thrive then what is the point? If they won't value their church they certainly won't value their ministry. And if you give ministry to one who has never tithed you are giving ministry to someone who is unreliable and who is eventually going to leave and create gaps in the ministry of the church.

It may be subconscious but people are tied into what they have invested in. When it comes to ministry it is more than the money they have given. It is that they feel a part of what they are in and as a result are more likely to take ministry seriously.

They want to see the bills paid, they want to see the church having impact and they want to see more church planting because they have invested in the house of God. They give because they are sold into the vision of our church and want to be a part of it. As important as finances are to the upkeep of the church, that aspect of giving is the most important part.

The day any church is given over to those who will not support it financially is the beginning of the end of that church. As much as they may like what we did they will not go out of their way to maintain it and give it a little bit of time and everything will collapse into the dust.

As long as we have people who invest into the vision we will have people who will continue to fight to maintain who we are as a church and as a fellowship. And believe me, in an age where churches are closing left, right and centre, that really matters.

# 8. WHY NO WINE?

If there is a standard in which we are seen by the religious world as putting a yoke on our congregation is our stance against alcohol. For some, we are seen as having gone too far.

Why can't we allow drinking in moderation? What's wrong with a beer now again or a glass of wine with our meals? Why can't we make merry at Christmas?

## ALCOHOL AND BRITISH CULTURE

These could be valid questions depending on who's doing the asking. That may seem like a snide comment but we live in a culture that is increasingly alcohol indulgent in nature. We live in a society where people do not drink in moderation but where they are looking, not only to get drunk, but to get absolutely hammered when they go out. Having a good time, it seems, means drinking to the point where we lose all our senses.

We live in a generation where drinking is the number one social activity. It doesn't help, of course, that alcohol is relatively cheap. It is possible in our day to get drunk for less than £5. At Christmas and at special sporting occasions the price of alcohol falls even lower! People may not realise this but pubs and restaurants are serving wine in larger glasses than before. There removal of certain laws that once curtailed drinking throughout the night has added to the increasing drunken behaviour of British youth.

One in four adults in Britain are binge drinkers with Britain being the recorded as Europe's heaviest alcohol consumers.[1] It is interesting to note that women are catching up with men when it comes to drinking. It has been recorded that the proportion of women who binge drink in Great Britain has increased from 8% in 1998 to 15% in 2006.[2]

The reality is that drinking to get drunk is a part of British culture and it is this worldly drinking culture that is seeking to establish itself in the modern church under the guise of being 'biblically allowed'.

## A LITTLE WINE FOR THE STOMACH'S SAKE

Now to answer the question honestly and especially for those who are sincerely looking for direction and understanding it must be pointed out that drinking is not necessarily a sin. I've mentioned this right off the bat because there is always some pro-alcohol Christian who is ready to quote 1 Timothy 5:23 which states, *"No longer drink only water, but use a little wine for your stomach's sake and your frequent infirmities."*

---

[1] http://www.dailymail.co.uk/health/article-302531/Special-report-Binge-drinking.html
[2] http://www.guardian.co.uk/society/2009/may/06/binge-drinking-women

There are a couple of points to note here. Paul wasn't against using 'a little wine' but it was for medicinal purposes and not recreational. But it also showed that 'a little wine' was not sin which is what the pro-alcohol Christian is looking to point out. Though that is true what we also need to see is that up until that point Timothy was a teetotaller. He did have a stand against alcohol and Paul's suggestion was not for him to disregard his conviction but to recognise the medicinal purposes 'a little wine' could do. It wasn't for him now to spend his weekends on the town frequenting the various taverns and inns. However, the idea of 'a little wine' shows that alcohol is not a sin but drunkenness is.

Before we go further we need to recognise we cannot view or judge a different time and place with the spectacles of this day and age. For example, fourteenth century king of Scotland Robert the Bruce, at the age of sixteen married Elizabeth de Burgh who was twelve at the time. Twenty six year old poet Edgar Allen Poe married his thirteen year old cousin Virginia in 1835. People may view this as abhorrent but that was a different time and age when life expectancy was much lower than it is today.

The same is true when we consider the issue of alcohol. Alcohol then and now is not necessarily the same thing. We live in an age of technology where things are made on an incredible scale. We have things that are mass produced and what was once rare or expensive in the olden days are relatively cheap today because of our technological advances.

This is seen in the creation of alcohol. Today we have factories that are not only huge in size but are actually very efficient in extracting alcohol from fermenting sugar cane, grapes and other materials. As a result alcohol is mass produced on a scale never seen before in world history and in many places cheaper than it has ever been. Today one can go to a local store and get wines produced as far as South Africa, Chile and Australia. Alcohol is big business.

In our generation there are many types of alcohol that people drink, for example, beer, wine, vodka, rum, champagne, whiskey and so on. In the bible there is only one drink worthy of note and that is – wine. Interestingly, while wine means only one thing in our language and culture, in the bible, the word 'wine' has many different meanings in its original Hebrew. Thus the question needs to be asked, *"Is the wine of today the same as the wine in ancient times?"*

## BIRDS OF A FEATHER

For example, there is 'yayin' which means 'fermented wine'. It is the word used of Noah in Genesis 9:21 which says, *"Then he drank of the wine and was drunk, and became uncovered in his tent."*

Then there is 'tiyrosh' which means 'fresh grape juice' or 'grape juice just squeezed out'. This is seen in the words Isaac spoke to his son Esau concerning Jacob in Genesis 27:37 which states, *"Then Isaac answered and said to Esau, "Indeed I have made him your master, and all his brethren I have given to him as servants; with grain and wine I have sustained him."* It is also translated as 'new wine'. So, it is clear to see that this is non-alcoholic wine.

There is another word used for 'alcohol' in the Hebrew and that is 'shekar' which is usually translated as 'intoxicating drink' or as the King James Version would have it – 'strong drink'. Isaiah 5:22 states, *"Woe to men mighty at drinking wine* (yayin), *woe to men valiant for mixing intoxicating drink* (shekar)..."

Notice that wine ('yayin') and intoxicating drink ('shekar') always go hand in hand.

1 Samuel 1:15 - But Hannah answered and said, "No, my lord, I am a woman of sorrowful spirit. I have drunk neither _wine_ nor _intoxicating drink_, but have poured out my soul before the Lord.

Isaiah 29:9 - They are drunk, but not with _wine_; they stagger, but not with _intoxicating drink_.

Isaiah 56:12 - "Come," one says, "I will bring _wine_, and we will fill ourselves with _intoxicating drink_;

Micah 2:11 - If a man should walk in a false spirit and speak a lie, saying, 'I will prophesy to you of _wine_ and _drink_,' even he would be the prattler of this people.

This shows us three things: (a) wine ('yayin'), although alcoholic, is not the same as 'intoxicating drink ('shekar'); (b) wine is not as potent as intoxicating drink; and (c) the fact that they are shown together shows that they are birds of a feather as they are both alcoholic in nature. As a matter of fact they are seen as partners in crime all throughout scripture.

Leviticus 10:8-9 - Then the Lord spoke to Aaron, saying: "Do not drink _wine_ or _intoxicating drink_, you, nor your sons with you, when you go into the tabernacle of meeting, lest you die. It shall be a statute forever throughout your generations

Judges 13:4 - Now therefore, please be careful not to drink _wine_ or similar _drink_.

Proverbs 20:1 - **_Wine_** is a mocker, **_strong drink_** is a brawler, and whoever is led astray by it is not wise.

Proverbs 31:4 - It is not for kings, O Lemuel, it is

not for kings to drink _**wine**_, nor for princes _**intoxicating drink**_;

Proverbs 31:6 – Give _**strong drink**_ to him who is perishing, and _**wine**_ to those who are bitter of heart.

Isaiah 5:11 – Woe to those who rise early in the morning, that they may follow _**intoxicating drink**_; who continue until night, till _**wine**_ inflames them!

Isaiah 28:7 – But they also have erred through _**wine**_, and through _**intoxicating drink**_ are out of the way; the priest and the prophet have erred through _**intoxicating drink**_, they are swallowed up by _**wine**_, they are out of the way through _**intoxicating drink**_; they err in vision, they stumble in judgment.

## A LOOK FROM ANCIENT TIMES

From these scriptures we see that the Bible really frowns on the use of wine because of its ability to lead people to drunkenness. Yet not only did the Bible frown on drunkenness but also, with people of ancient times as well, wine wasn't drunk undiluted unless one wanted to get drunk.

Professor Robert H Stein wrote an article in Christianity Today called "Wine Drinking in the New Testament Times". In it he states:

> "What is important for us to note is that before wine was drunk it was mixed with water....The ratio of water to wine varied. Homer *(Odyssey* IX, 208f.) mentions a ratio of 20 to 1, twenty parts water to one part wine. Pliny *(Natural History* XIV, vi, 54) mentions a ratio of eight parts water to one part wine. In one ancient work, Athenaeus's *The Learned*

*Banquet,* written around A.D. 200, we find in Book Ten a collection of statements from earlier writers about drinking practices. A quotation from a play by Aristophanes reads: "'Here, drink this also, mingled three and two.' DEMUS. 'Zeus! But it's sweet and bears the three parts well!'"

The poet Euenos, who lived in the fifth century B.C., is also quoted:

*The best measure of wine is neither much nor very little;*

*For 'tis the cause of either grief or madness.*

*It pleases the wine to be the fourth, mixed with three nymphs.*

Here the ratio of water to wine is 3 to 1. Others mentioned are:

    3 to 1 — Hesiod

    4 to 1 — Alexis

    2 to 1 — Diodes

    3 to 1 — Ion

    5 to 2 — Nichochares

    2 to 1 — Anacreon

Sometimes the ratio goes down to 1 to 1 (and even lower), but it should be noted that such a mixture is referred to as "strong wine." Drinking wine unmixed, on the other hand, was looked upon as a "Scythian" or barbarian custom.

Athenaeus in this work quotes Mnesitheus of Athens:

> The gods has revealed wine to mortals, to be the greatest blessing for those who use it aright, but for those who use it without measure, the reverse. For it gives food to them that take it and strength in mind and body. In medicine it is most beneficial; it can be mixed with liquid and drugs and it brings aid to the wounded. In daily intercourse, to those who mix and drink it moderately, it gives good cheer; but if you overstep the bounds, it brings violence. Mix it half and half, and you get madness; unmixed, bodily collapse.

It is evident that wine was seen in ancient times as a medicine (and as a solvent for medicines) and of course as a beverage. Yet as a beverage it was always thought of as a mixed drink. Plutarch *(Symposiacs* III, ix), for instance, states. "We call a mixture 'wine,' although the larger of the component parts is water." The ratio of water might vary, but only barbarians drank it unmixed, and a mixture of wine and water of equal parts was seen as "strong drink" and frowned upon. The term "wine" or *oinos* in the ancient world, then, did not mean wine as we understand it today but wine mixed with water. Usually a writer simply referred to the mixture of water and wine as "wine." To indicate that the beverage was not a mixture of water and wine he would say "unmixed *(akratesteron)* wine."

... In ancient times there were not many beverages that were safe to drink. The danger of drinking water alone raises another point. There were several ways in which the ancients could make water safe to drink. One method was boiling, but this was tedious and costly. Different methods of filtration were tried. The safest and easiest method of making the water safe to drink, however, was to mix it with wine. The drinking of wine (i.e., a mixture of water and wine) served therefore as a safety measure, since often the water available was not safe.

We in the western world take it for granted to have clean running water through our taps. It never crosses our minds that even to this day many people still get their water from contaminated wells and streams. Perhaps this is what Paul was alluding to when he spoke to his disciple Timothy as wine ('yayin') was often added to water to improve its quality.

But today's society is completely different to life in biblical times as we have so many alternatives to drinking wine as a means of staying healthy while being hydrated. Supermarkets are filled with juices, water, teas, coffees, milks, diluted and 'just add water' drinks. We have so many choices available to us that we have no need to drink wine. We would have to find ourselves in the backside of a wilderness somewhere in the third world to justify drinking wine in an attempt to keep ourselves from drinking contaminated water.

## RISE ABOVE IT

Not only is there no need in drinking alcohol in this day and age but we are also inviting trouble when we open the door to alcoholic drinks. The book of Proverbs points out repeatedly the dangers of drinking alcohol. Proverbs 20:1 says, *"Wine is a mocker, strong drink is a* brawler, and whoever is led astray by it is not wise." Proverbs 31:4 declares, "It is not for kings, O Lemuel, it is not for kings to drink wine, nor for princes intoxicating drink."

Proverbs 31:6 shocks us by saying, "Give strong drink to him who is perishing, and wine to those who are bitter of heart."

From these scriptures we see that alcohol is to be frowned upon. They show that alcohol leads people astray and those who drink it have no wisdom or discernment. The scriptures frown upon alcohol because it shows it to be a negative thing that leads people to do negative things. It also shows in no uncertain terms that alcohol is for LOSERS and for people so wrecked by life that have no desire to go on. It informs us that people who have a sense of dignity and self-worth are to stay clear from alcohol as it has the ability to ruin lives.

That right there should be enough to stop people from drinking but there are always some people who feel that they have the ability to *'drink in moderation'* or *'drink and not get drunk'*. By one useless cliché they have managed to underestimate the power of alcohol and overestimate their powers of self-control.

## DRINKING IN MODERATION IS SELF-DECEPTION

I was not saved in a Potter's House Church and for the six of the first eight months of my salvation I went to a Baptist church where almost everyone, including the pastor, drank alcohol. Again the clichés were used: *'drink in moderation'* and *'drink and not get drunk'*.

The church building was across the road from the pub and after every Sunday morning service people from the church would take the nine or ten steps needed to enter the pub. I can remember as a new Christian going to the youth leader's apartment and seeing outside littered with Fosters beer cans and her waking up to a serious hangover. Even then I knew that this wasn't right and that Christians ought not to be drinking.

A few years later, a few of us from the Potter's House Church in South London had a fellowship at a restaurant called Texas Embassy. While there Cheryl (my wife) and I saw a certain young lady from our old church who was a member of the praise and worship team. She was a nurse who happened to be on a hen night and she was absolutely drunk out of her mind. Later on we ended up in Leicester Square only to find this young lady and her friends completely out of their minds laughing, screaming, stumbling and falling over themselves.

I remember Cheryl going over to her and reminding her that she was a Christian and that she had a testimony of exampleship to remember. Instead of thanks Cheryl was met with a volley of abuse. That night was a great revelation to me as those words *'drink in moderation'* and *'drink and not get drunk'* came back to mind. It made me recognise that those words are really words of fantasy as sooner or later, whether your guard is down or because you are going through a rough patch or whatever, if you drink alcohol you will eventually get drunk. It is inevitable. One day Satan is going to exploit that and all it takes is one night of drunkenness to tear down years of Christian testimony.

Alcohol drinking inevitably leads to decadence. The word 'decadence' has its roots in the word 'decay'. It is no coincidence that alcohol is a product of decay. When sugars decay they become alcohol. That is why anyone who eats an old piece of sugar cane will recognise the taste as being similar to rum because it is diluted rum. Eat enough of this cane and you will find yourself drunker than a skunk.

We need to remember as well that death and decay only came into the world because of Adam's sin. Thus, if we are to believe the bible, alcohol could not exist in a sinless world because there would have been no decay and hence no decadence.

Isn't it shocking that Noah, a preacher of righteousness, a man who lived for God in a generation of unrighteousness, who went about patiently building an ark in the middle of nowhere embracing the insults, mocking and abuse of his heathen neighbours and finally surviving the judgment of the whole earth, after the flood built a vineyard, made the equivalent of what Americans called 'moonshine' and got himself so drunk that he ran around naked. After doing so much for God it was a real disappointment reading that about Noah.

Or what about Lot, again another righteous man who was oppressed at the unrighteous conduct of his neighbours, but the last we read of him he was in a cave where his daughters got him so drunk on two occasions that he committed incest with them. If that isn't decadence then I don't know what is.

It is so clear from the word of God that these two men recognised by the bible as being righteous ended up damaging their testimony because of alcohol drinking. Did they mean for that to happen? I don't think so but that's what alcohol does when you indulge in it. You never know just how far you are going to go.

How many times have well respected people been shamed and embarrassed because of a one-off drunken spree? How many work relationships have been compromised by an office party at Christmas? Marriages have ended in divorce, businesses ruined, employment lost, reputation destroyed and lives shattered, not necessarily of habitual alcoholism but one moment of drunken madness.

## ALCOHOL RUINS OUR TESTIMONY

Our power as Christians do not stem from the words we speak but the life we live. It takes years to build up a godly reputation based upon character yet it takes only a few minutes to completely tear that same reputation down. Being in ministry means that we represent our church and our behaviour reflects the church whether we like it or not.

There are many people who are convicted of their sins and as a result sigh in relief when they see a prominent Christian drunk or doing something they are not expected to be doing.

I remember reading a book years ago where the author told of an occasion where he witnessed to an acquaintance about his need to become a Christian. The acquaintance was so moved that he promised to go to church with the author the next Sunday. It just so happened that on the Saturday afternoon the author was down at his local pub drinking a pint when in walked the acquaintance. After an awkward minute the acquaintance said, *"I guess I don't need to go to church with you tomorrow after all."*

## ALCOHOL NULLIFIES OUR EXAMPLESHIP

Not only are there honest people who are looking for a godly example to follow and rebellious sinners looking to point fingers at the 'hypocrites' in church there are also many men and women coming into our churches who are struggling with alcohol addictions. The best thing for them is to be in an environment where alcohol is completely off limits. Wouldn't such people be embolden to drink when they see established saints in ministry knocking back shots of tequila at a fellowship or finishing off cases of beer watching a football game? And let us assume that we can drink without getting drunk yet for some of these people one drop of alcohol annihilates months of hard work staying off the wagon.

I have seen personally just how hard it is for some people to stay sober. I have seen people with great potential figuratively pee their lives down the toilet and destroy themselves because of alcohol addiction. We have a great responsibility as the church of God and as examples of Christianity to make a personal stand against the evils of alcohol by avoiding it completely.

Once again I would like to make it clear that this isn't an issue of salvation but it is an issue of Christian exampleship and it is a critical issue in this day and age. The apostle Paul rightfully said in Romans 14:21, *"It is good neither to eat meat nor drink wine nor do anything by which your brother stumbles or is offended or is made weak."*

## USING JESUS AS AN EXCUSE

Right about now someone may want to interject and say, *"Well then, why did Jesus turn water into wine?"* To answer that question simply and quickly, we must consider the fact that wine as seen in the bible could mean either alcoholic or non-alcoholic. If it is alcoholic then we must ask ourselves the question *"Why would Jesus turn water into something that could cause people to get drunk?"*

We must remember that the miracle of turning water into wine only occurred when the other wine was already finished. John 2:10 recalls the words of the Master of Ceremonies to the bridegroom, *"And he said to him, "Every man at the beginning sets out the good wine, and when the guests have well drunk, then the inferior. You have kept the good wine until now!"*

If the wine was alcoholic and *"the guests have well drunk"* it means turning the water into the good wine was more than likely to cause the guests to become drunk. I mean, if people are already saturated with wine and now they taste some really good stuff they are more than likely to come back for more and in the end get drunk. That means Jesus purposely created a stumbling block for people but knowing the righteous character of Christ it means that it would have been impossible for Him to have done so.

Consider, if a man has had a history of beating up his wife, the next time we see his wife sporting a black eye and she says that she walked into a door we can all safely conclude with reasonable accuracy that her husband did it and she is covering up for him. However, if a man has been married to his wife for fifty years and had always treated her with respect and dignity with his children, family and friends testifying that they have never seen him lay a hand on her, if we see her sporting a black eye and she said that she walked into a door we can all safely conclude with reasonable accuracy that she indeed walked into a door.

How much more Jesus who is the very Word of God? How can the One who wrote against drunkenness be the very agent of the thing He so fiercely opposes?

Not to mention that Jesus is the Author of life and if He is the Author of life how can He turn water into the decaying product called alcohol. How can the Creator of life create something that is literally the product of death and corruption? Without question, the wine transformed by Jesus from the water was in fact fresh grape juice. So fresh that the Master of Ceremonies was impressed by it!

# IT IS WHAT IT IS

As Christians we should let the word of God be our guide. Rather than try and find loopholes to justify sinful desires we should take it for what it is. Proverbs 20:1 says, *"Wine is a mocker, strong drink is a brawler, and whoever is led astray by it is not wise."* How much clearer can the Scriptures be? And for a Bible verse that is nearly 3,000 years old it hits so close to home in our society today.

Consider that in the year 2010, 40% of patients admitted to Accident and Emergency (A&E) departments across Britain are alcohol related injuries or illnesses. Consider that traffic accidents are the leading cause of alcohol related deaths in young men between the ages of 16-24. Consider that one in ten fatal accidents in the home is alcohol related. Consider that one third of people who die in household fires have been drinking. Consider that 14% of children are being brought up in a family where at least one adult has a drinking problem.[3]

The impact of alcohol really hit home years ago when I was living in Manchester. One Saturday night, after coming back from an impact team, the driver and I went to drop the minibus back to the rental agency. We had to drive through Manchester City Centre at about 2am. I had never seen such a commotion on these streets ever. These same streets that I outreached on, that I've shopped on, that I've gone to restaurants on were like on a different world.

There were a number of fights mostly between men but one between two women. There were people were vomiting in the middle of the road and people staggering

---

[3] http://www.guardian.co.uk/society/2011/jan/31/drink-survey-cost-alcohol-abuse

in the streets. Shouts of obscenity and curses were broadcasted through the air from one part of town to the next. It was complete chaos and boy, were we glad to get home that night.

Just from a practical rational view on alcohol we can see its destructive nature at work in individuals. For one, alcohol turns people into monsters. There are people who are mild mannered as they come but with one bout of drinking all of a sudden become violent creatures. How many husbands and wives live in fear of an alcohol abusing spouse? How many children live in fear of an alcohol abusing parent? We see the damage cocaine, heroin and crack can cause and we avoid it and preach against it yet why can't we see the damage alcohol does and do the same?

Secondly and related quite closely to our first reason, alcohol makes many innocent victims. Along with innocent spouses and children, how many innocent people have been randomly attacked by drunks? We are reading of increasing incidents of people being beaten to death by drunken youths. There have been countless times I've read of innocent individuals minding their own business who've ended up with a broken pint glass smashed into their eye leaving them blind.

Thirdly and quite related to our second reason, alcohol leaves people vulnerable to attack. How many drunken individuals are easy targets for criminals? It's so easy to rob them of their coats, shoes and wallets. Even more disturbing, how many drunken women are easy targets for predators. How many young women are so plastered out of their minds that they literally lie unconscious in the streets or on benches? A major study by the Association of Chief Police Officers found that the majority of women who claim to be victims of a date-rape drug like Rohypnol or Gammahydroxybutrate (GHB) are in fact under the influence of alcohol.

Fourthly, we need to remember that alcohol brings out the worst in us. Is it too much for me to say that wherever alcohol is present sin is not far behind? Alcohol makes people drop their inhibitions and do things that they would never do in a million years. Alcohol leads to violence, verbal and physical abuse, immoral acts and sexual immorality. Like I said before, alcohol breeds decadence. In an article in the Daily Mail, Dr Sarah Jarvis, of the Royal College of General Practitioners, said: *"We have known for years that excessive alcohol use is linked to unprotected sex which can increase the risk of catching sexually transmitted infections."*

I could go on and on and on but the point is clear. There is not much good in alcohol and as Christians doing our best to live exemplary lives, we should stay far from it.

## NO NEED FOR WINE AS A MEDICINE

Like I pointed out before, we live in such an age of luxury. We have water coming through our taps. Instead of hiking miles out into the forest somewhere to get water for the family to use we can simply roll out of bed and into the kitchen to make a cup of tea with the cleanest water since Adam and Eve. You can go into your local supermarket and if it pleases you, you can get an assortment of water from different parts of the world. If plain water isn't your forte there are so many different types of fruit drinks available from so many different brands. You can choose from Capri Sun, Five Alive, Ribena, Tropical Rhythm, Grace, Tru Juice, etc. You can have grape, apple, mango, apple & mango, grapefruit, orange, orange & mango, blackcurrant, fruit punch, exotic fruits, etc. At ASDA you can get four one litre boxes for £3.

In our day and age there is absolutely no need to drink alcohol! Absolutely none whatsoever. There is so much to enjoy without us having to pay the price of losing our minds. Let us leave this abusive concoction of hell for those who have no desire for God. Let those who are righteous look towards the new wine we will drink at the wedding feast of the Lamb.

## 9. TV OR NOT TV?

**(That is the question)**


Apart from sin, the bane of effective ministry is entertainment, and in particular television.

Now I must mention that there are some who are of the belief that the Potter's House Church teaches that anyone who owns a television is not saved. That is not true. What we teach is a warning against the owning of the television as it not only damages the effectiveness of Christian ministry but it can also destroy the moral compass of believers.

It would be impossible, not to mention going further than our authority allows, in banning everyone who steps through our church doors from having a television. For one, you can take away television from people's living rooms but you can't take it out of their hearts. It has to be a genuine conviction on the part of an ordinary Christian for them not to have a television.

Instead we warn people and inform people of the dangers of television ownership. There are three main reasons why television is a hot bed of spiritual danger.

## SATAN'S PULPIT: THE SUBTLE WORK OF DEMONIC PROPAGANDA

Firstly, television whether you like it or not, is more than an instrument of entertainment. Television uses entertainment as a means to educate people to the values of those who control it. There are people who hate coming to church because their excuse is that they don't like being preached to. These same people are clueless to the fact that every day they are being preached to. They may not be preached to in the local church but they are definitely being preached to in the comfort of their own home.

People in general are afraid of cults controlling how they think yet they are completely blind to the biggest cult leader in the world sitting in their living room! Television tells us what to eat, what to wear, what is morally acceptable, what is in fashion, how to spend our time, etc.

Bob Pittman, the founder of MTV, made these shocking words a few years ago: *"We don't shoot for the fourteen year olds. We own them!"* This is not an empty boast. Statistics show that teenagers rely more on television than school to teach them about life. They copy the clothes, personalities and hairstyles of the celebrities they watch on television.

The power of television lies in the fact that it instantly lowers our guard. We can sit blissfully in front of a television unaware as to the fact that we are being preached to. As we watch our favourite soap, cartoon, movie or even documentary we are either blatantly or subtly being instructed in the doctrines and teachings of this world.

These doctrines are taught over and over again, not necessarily in the same program but eventually these ideas do stick in our heads. The agenda behind television is all about thoughts and suggestions. It is to put thoughts and suggestions in your mind and not only for you to think of them but to make them your own. The sad thing is that there are a lot of people who believe that the thoughts they think are really their own not realising that they have been put there by television.

A touching story of two homosexuals in love but persecuted by ignorant people moves us into embracing perversion as another type of love. A creative documentary using modern CGI technology 'recreates' how dinosaurs used to live and so dismisses the biblical account of creation. A cartoon about a rebellious teenager and his idiot father makes us accept that rebellion is acceptable. A weekly series about a teenage witch shows us that sorcery is nothing to be afraid of.

Right now someone may be saying that I must think that people in general are fools for just falling for anything simply because of a television program says so. But if you consider the fact that the average person watches more than four hours of television each day, which computes to about two months of non-stop television watching a year, then you can see that if someone growing up from a young child to adulthood will receive most of their training from what they watch on television.

When I bought my house back in 2004 the previous owner had a television complete with a stand in all four bedrooms, the storage room at the back of the house and the living room. That is six televisions in one house.

Hour after hour, week after week and month after

month, the messages being preached by television is being drummed in the brains of those whose guards have been let down. The art of propaganda is that if you keep hearing something over and over and over again pretty soon it starts to sink it and it becomes a reality in your mind.

Have you ever gone through a situation where you are explaining something you learned to someone only for them to turn around and tell you, *"I told you that"*? All that time you thought it was you who created your own 'thinks' when in reality someone had 'thought' it for you! How much is that true in life in general? How is it that in recent years there has been such a paradigm shift in thought? Back in the 1970s it was illegal to be a homosexual and today in 2010s it is illegal to speak against homosexuality. Why were people anti-homosexual then and pro-homosexual now?

## THE DEMONIC STRATEGY OF THOUGHTS AND SUGGESTIONS

If you fail to blame the media and primarily television then there is something wrong with you. Television isn't content to entertain you with meaningless drivel. Television is hell bent (no pun intended) on controlling the way you think by implanting thoughts and suggestions that you eventually think are yours by way of origin.

Ultimately television is Satan's tool. The devil's plan was always to plant thoughts and suggestions in the minds of the people in order to get them to do what he wants them to do.

Consider Adam and Eve who were fine with God's will and purposes until Satan came and implanted certain thoughts and suggestions.

Genesis 3:1 says, *"Now the serpent was more cunning than any beast of the field which the Lord God had made. And he said to the woman, "Has God indeed said, 'You shall not eat of every tree of the garden'?""*

The very first strategy used by Satan in undermining man and God's will for his life was to implant thoughts and suggestions. Satan has not changed his strategy as it still works very well. In our generation Satan still speaks through television and his suggestions are *"Is homosexuality really a sin?" "Did God really create the earth?" "Why should you listen to your parents?" "Is witchcraft really a big deal?"*

These are just the handful of thoughts that Satan subtly suggests to people oblivious to his strategy. Thoughts that would have never had otherwise entered into the minds of people. Can you imagine the amount of 'preaching' people listen to on a daily basis? Can you imagine the amount of 'doctrine' that is being hammered into people's minds repeatedly?

The majority of people are completely unaware and unsuspecting to the fact that they are being brainwashed by a demonic strategy. The irony doesn't fail to escape me as these same people would look at us and consider us to be brainwashed by the Bible.

The truth be known is that ultimately we get our 'thoughts' from either one of two sources – God or Satan. It all comes down to two scriptures we see in the lives of Adam and Eve and that is – *"...God said..."* and *"...the serpent said..."*

In our generation the television has been hijacked by the unwitting agents of Satan in order to push his thoughts and suggestions into our oblivious minds.

# HOLLYWOOD IS DEMONICALLY INSPIRED

At the turn of the twenty-first century, family oriented movie distributers like CleanFlicks, CleanFilms, CleanVideo and Family Flix USA began to be formed. These were companies that edited films in order to remove swearing, nudity and other morally unsound elements. Due to the efforts of these companies you could get a modern day film on DVD that was completely free from morally unsavoury parts.

However, Hollywood was outraged. Entertainment studios such as Disney (yes, Disney), Sony, Universal, Paramount and Twentieth Century Fox along with prominent directors such as Steven Spielberg and Robert Redford sued these companies in 2002 and in the next three to four years they all were shut down by the federal courts in the USA.

Daniel Thompson, owner of four CleanFlicks shops in Utah said, *"I think it is ridiculous that you can't watch a movie without seeing sex, nudity or extreme violence. I don't understand why they are trying to keep that in there."* [4]

The reason is, Daniel, there is an agenda to twist the moral fabric of society by using entertainment. On the face of it, there doesn't seem to be much reason to have these elements in but that's because the television has been hijacked to corrupt the minds of people.

This leads to the second reason why television is a menace to Christianity. The majority of television is geared towards sexual perversion, violence, immorality and the elevation of evil. Consider just how insidious television is when prime time television consists on watching the

---

[4] http://articles.latimes.com/2006/jul/10/business/fi-clean10

solving of all types of gruesome murders.

Whether it is sin or not isn't the issue but recently there has been a proliferation of television crime series: CSI: Las Vegas, CSI: Miami, and CSI: New York. Then there is Law & Order: Special Victims Unit, Law & Order: Criminal Intent, etc. Then there is 'Lost without a trace' 'Cold Case', etc. The list just goes on and on and on.

(Interestingly, there is something called the CSI effect in which one of the manifestations is the increased popularity in forensic science programs at universities across the world. According to a BBC report, in 1991 there were only two first-class degree courses in forensic science but today there are more than 400. Talk about television influencing people.)

Recent statistics show that the average young person will have watched 200,000 violent acts including 16,000 murders by the time he or she graduates from high school.

Then we have the reality television programs such as Big Brother whose producers are desperate for all kinds of shenanigans to go on so that it boosts up attendance ratings. Finding the off-scouring of Britain and putting them in one room is television's idea to great entertainment.

I can remember growing up in the 80s and many people were making complaints at the moral decadence of MTV. Being an unsaved teen I used to wonder what's wrong with these people but the reality is that MTV, VH-1 and stations like this were mild in the 80s in comparison to today. Going to the gym for a work out can be a real struggle when you see the likes of Beyonce and Rihanna shaking their 'thing' on the twenty or so television screens all across the gym.

Then there are the beloved soaps which dishes out every kind of filth imaginable to keep viewers hooked. Bad enough to feature the age old spectacle of adultery we now live in a day where stations are fighting to show the first lesbian or gay kiss.

Even if you manage to find something clean and wholesome you also have to navigate your way through the commercials. These perhaps may be the most insidious of the lot. Why does it take sex to advertise deodorant? Just tell me how this brand of deodorant is effective in stopping bad smells from coming from my arm pits! Why are men put down so many times in order to advertise flights or crisps or corn flakes? Why do we need sexual innuendo to sell chocolate? That just sells itself!

Almost two-thirds of the scenes in prime time television include some reference to sex. Twenty-eight percent of these will put the primary emphasis on sex. And when intercourse takes place, it is four to eight times as likely to occur between unmarried couples as between a husband and wife.

How many prime time television programs can you see that promote family values? Why is it that every family is going through a divorce or have an absentee parent? Why is there a necessity for actors to swear? Why is there a constant attack on the 9pm watershed? Why is it that the programs that are featured before 9pm not much better than those after 9pm. After all, Eastenders and Coronation Street and all the other soaps (ironic to be called 'soap') are shown well before 9pm and have many children who are following every single detail.

I could be going on for pages speaking about all the evils television is responsible for pumping into our living room but the one question that should make you realise that evil is the main ingredient of television is this: *"How much of Christianity is seen in modern television?"* The answer is that there isn't much. Apart from the meek and mild 'Songs of Praise' on BBC for half an hour on Sundays there isn't much more. Maybe at night somewhere around 2am to 4am they may show a documentary about the history of Christianity.

But even then these documentaries challenge the authority of the Bible and promote more questioning of the Bible rather than answers. If a film is shown it is usually something blasphemous or close to it. How much preaching do you see on television? How much time is allocated to discuss Christian faith and values? Let's face the facts – television in Britain is hostile to Christianity.

Yet we invite, without hesitation, such a blatant enemy of Christ into our homes every day.

## THE ART OF DISTRACTION

The third reason may be the most insidious of the lot. With the proliferation of cable television it is possible to select certain stations as a possible playlist. We could have National Geographic, BBC News 24, Sky News, Sky Sports, Discovery, Cartoon Network and other mild stations where we see nothing of immorality, sexual innuendo, and so on.

But right here we face another monster called 'distraction'. Distraction along with sin is the main strategy of Satan in the fight against effectiveness. If Satan can keep you distracted he can keep you from being effective. How many of us have been at one time or the other distracted by television watching? You had somewhere important to go but something very interesting came on the television? Maybe it was on Great White Sharks on the reefs of Australia? It could have been on animal migration in the

Serengeti? What about a top story or breaking news on the news channel? And as a result of being distracted you were late for something very important or you never studied the way you could for your exam and you got a 'B' instead of an 'A'.

I have known of people who point blank refuse to come to church because of their commitment to certain programs on a Sunday evening. It is the distraction of entertainment that hinders so many people from coming to Christ. I have been to the deepest parts of central Africa where not much entertainment is found. One gospel film being shown on a Saturday night has the ability draw hundreds to hear the message of salvation. It is powerful to see so many hands being lifted up and people praying to get saved.

Coming back to Britain and being stirred about film evangelisation we get the church excited and with prayer and fasting and handing out thousands of flyers we expect people to come flooding into our church building to watch 'Lay it down' or 'Left Behind' only to find one or two people trickling in and who barely last the length of the film. Why? Most people are distracted with what is going on television on a Saturday night and are too tied in with what they are doing to come to some church and watch a film.

As Christians owning a television and giving ourselves to it will desensitise us to godly morals and convictions that are essential in having impact for the kingdom of God. But it also distracts us from being involved in more important things like praying, reading a book, fellowshipping or evangelisation.

In David Wilkerson's book 'The Cross and the Switchblade' he spoke about the occasion where he made the conscious decision that he was going to give up his television in order to make time to pray more and to relax and reflect before starting the new week on Monday. It would be his habit that after going to church on a Sunday evening that when he got home he would relax by watching some television before going to bed.

The first night, however, he picked up a newspaper to read and saw the case of gang members who were being caught up in a murder investigation. He was so moved by what he saw that he went to the court case and as a result of that made up his mind to reach inner city youth for Jesus Christ. That was the beginning of the Teen Challenge ministry and overnight David Wilkerson turned from an insignificant country preacher into an international revivalist. Imagine if he had not made the decision to get rid of his television? He would still be in obscurity today.

Now I'm not saying that everyone who gets rid of their television will have an international ministry but the point being made is that without the distraction of a television God can speak more clearly to you and you can have more of a spiritual impact for God.

How many people can't get up in the morning and pray before they go to work because they were up so late the night before watching a program they did not expect to watch. You knew better, you knew that in the morning it would be very difficult to get up but you talk yourself out of the truth in order to be entertained only for you to get up and not be able to pray or have a devotional time with God. How many Christians know that their spiritual lives could be better if they weren't so distracted by television watching?

How many Christians are distracted from their families because of television? I remember years ago, while pioneering in Manchester, a married couple coming to church whose marriage was severely strained. They literally had no communication with each other. A few months passed and behold the television broke down and the wife came to me in joy that next Sunday that she and her husband had the best talk in years. Sadly, a few days later the television was repaired and that couple soon left church and today they are divorced. I'm sure there were many factors but I know for a fact that television was one of them.

Television is such a distraction that people at home are virtual strangers and parents have no clue as to what their children are up to as Dad is watching the Sopranos, Mom is watching Eastenders and the kids are watching the Simpsons. No longer do family members relate and when young Johnny gets in trouble at school the old familiar cry goes up, *"Not my Johnny. He's a good boy!"*

Margaret Mead, an anthropologist, makes a very interesting statement. *"Modern westerners have invented prisons for their children – bassinette, bouncinette, playpen and then television. In other cultures (for example, traditional Chinese families), children spend a lot more time sitting on their parents' knee. As a result, western TV kids more alienated from their parents. In the traditional culture children are far more loyal to their parents' value."*

I've been to visit Christians only to be left in the living room with the kids watching television while they go off to make me a cup of tea and to be honest I've been shocked at what these Christian parents have allowed their children to watch. It is either these parents are so desensitised by years of television watching that they can't discern right from wrong anymore or just as terrible, they have not stopped to monitor what young Johnny and Suzy are watching.

It is thought provoking but how much time do we spend with our children educating them on the things of God and right living in comparison to the time they spend watching television?

Television is such a distraction that Christian people who have been brought up on television can't even sit down and listen to a forty minute sermon. We live in a generation where people have a limited concentration span. We are so used to flashing lights, pulse racing action scenes, jokes, intrigue and drama that listening to a sermon seems boring in comparison.

As Christian ministers we need to be concerned about our effectiveness. To round up all that I've said before, watching vulgar movies can slowly desensitise you. If you give yourself to them you will slowly find yourself accepting things that once would cause you to be greatly convicted. After a while, swearing, sexual innuendo and nudity no longer offends you or violate your conscience like it used to.

And even if what we watch is 'harmless' it is so easy to get distracted that you spend all kinds of hours watching things you didn't plan on watching and in the end, because time is limited, it is your relationship with God that suffers. We are too tired in the morning to pray or to concentrate reading the word of God. You may fool yourself into thinking that you will make up for lost time later on but that time never comes. Before you know it a new day has started and you can't make up for it.

I would say it is almost impossible to have a television and be truly effective as a Christian. One would have to have discipline that is almost out of this world to be able to juggle a spiritual life and a television. You may think that you do but in all probability that is all that it is.

You think you do. Like so many, your judgment is eroded and you can't see it.

## ENTERTAINMENT OR EFFECTIVENESS

Ultimately we have two choices that are diametrically opposed to each other. It is either we choose the way of television and lose our effectiveness or we get rid of our television in order to strengthen our effectiveness. We can't have both. You may think you can but the reality is that if you choose to have a television you have rejected spiritual effectiveness.

Can you have a television and be saved? Absolutely! No question! Does it mean that if I have a television I have no effectiveness? I didn't say that but what you will find is that you are nowhere as effective as you could be. Can a 100 metre runner train and eat cheeseburgers all day? Absolutely! Can he still run fast? Of course! He can run faster than the ordinary untrained guy. But when it comes to facing the Usain Bolts, Tyson Gays and Asafa Powells of this world he will be blown away.

Salvation may be free but spiritual effectiveness is not. It comes at a price and the more effective you are as a Christian you can be absolutely sure that a steeper price has been paid.

The sad thing is that many Christians have deceived themselves into thinking that they can be highly effective without paying a price. They believe that there is a loophole somehow. But like everyone who has achieved in life, success and effectiveness comes at a cost. When we accept ministry in the church we are saying that we are prepared to pay that cost.

Wouldn't it be sad and disappointing if someone went to a restaurant, sat down, was handed a menu, saw what was on offer and the price, ordered the best food in the house and finally ate and drank. But when the bill comes, although he knew the price, begins to bellyache and complain that the price was too high and he is unwilling to pay. He demands to speak to the manager in an attempt to get him to lower the cost.

It would have been better for him to have looked at the menu in the window, see the price and say to himself, *"I'm not willing to pay such a price. I will go to the next restaurant."*

Ultimately the issue isn't what you are losing but what you are getting in return. The issue is, what is it that you truly value? Jesus said in Matthew 13:45-46, *"Again, the kingdom of heaven is like a merchant seeking beautiful pearls, who, when he had found one pearl of great price, went and sold all that he had and bought it."*

To the merchant the pearl was worth more to him that everything he had. He did not see pearl as a sacrifice and it did not pain him to give up all that he had for it. It would have only been a pain, if in his heart, he thought what he had was worth more than the pearl.

For some, that is the issue, the television is worth far more than spiritual effectiveness and so it pains them when this standard of ministry comes up because in their heart of hearts they don't see spiritual effectiveness as being more valuable than the entertainment they receive from television.

You can choose ministry over television but if you are not convinced in your heart, you will always feel like you have been cheated or robbed by the church. Over time it becomes a regretful burden rather than a godly conviction.

## CINEMA AND THE SPIRIT OF FELLOWSHIP

In closing, I want to make another point in regards to the cinema. Without trying to rehash what I have said earlier I want to make an additional point. What makes the cinema anathema to the local church is that it will kill the spirit of fellowship. Can you imagine if we were to relax the standard of cinema attendance? There will be cinema fellowships every week? On Fridays and Saturdays (who knows what other days of the week) the cinema will be the place primarily church teens and young adults will hang out.

Instead of godly fellowship where the things of God are being discussed, it will instantly be replaced by mind-numbing cinema watching where we all watch a film together and yet completely separate as each of us is in a different world. And when we do get out, instead of edifying fellowship all we will be talking about is the action scene or the romantic scene in the film. In a matter of a month our church, especially amongst our youth, will have a completely carnal atmosphere and the next generation of spiritual warriors will be slain by the sword of entertainment.

Instead of having an outreach or a concert or some sort of spiritual event to go to they will be hanging out at the cinema behaving just like the youth in the world. You may think that this sounds like the ranting of a religious madman but the day we relax our stands on the cinema is the day that discipleship and church planting goes to the dogs.

## THE LETTER VERSUS THE SPIRIT

Finally, I wish I didn't have to say all of this was standards our fellowship has to uphold. I wish as Christians we would develop our own convictions on this as there are things that are not necessarily standards that nevertheless impede our spiritual effectiveness. Without going into details, the music we listen do can have an adverse affect on our spiritual lives. Without painting all secular music with one brush I have to say that much of modern music has the ability to dull our spiritual lives and hinder our effectiveness.

We may not have a standard that says that we must not listen to Fifty Cents or Lady Gaga but if you value spiritual effectiveness you will not allow such things to invade your personal life.

The issue ultimately isn't so much television, cinema, music, video games and so on but a self-cultivated desire to be on fire for God and to be spiritually effective in His kingdom. It doesn't have to be a standard. Just because the fellowship doesn't have a policy on certain things doesn't mean that it should be okay with us in regards to sacrificing spiritual effectiveness. The law of the Spirit goes further than the law of the letter. We ought not to miss the point by making the letter our focus and not the spirit.

# 10. WELCOME TO MY PARLOUR SAID THE SPIDER TO THE FLY

The Internet has been a revolutionary invention that has changed the face of the earth. It has literally permeated every area of life whether it is socially, academically, financially, etc. The list goes on.

## THE BENEFITS OF THE INTERNET

The Internet for a fact has made life far easier. For those who are nostalgic for the good old days the reality is you never had it so good. No longer do I need to queue at the bank when I can access my account online. As a matter of fact my financial activities don't need to come to an end on the weekends.

I can get directions to my destination, book a hotel in advance and find out the best restaurants in the area. At the click of a button I can order a book, pay my bills or purchase a flight ticket. I can even do my shopping done online!

Programs such as Skype allow me to talk and SEE

friends and family overseas for free. I can catch up on sports results half-way across the planet. I can find the latest news in the most remote regions of the world.

I no longer have to wait for weeks to send or receive documents but in an instant these things can be done over the Internet via email. The Internet has done much to keep us updated and gone are the days when we could not be in touch with vital news as this is the day of instant messaging.

How easy we forget that it was only a few years ago that if we wanted to buy something like a used book that we had to dig through the phone book for second hand book stores and call complete strangers only to be given the run around.

But with the Internet all we have to do is to tap in the name of the book on Google or check second hand book stores online and presto! The book is found!

The truth is that I can do so many things without leaving my front door saving me huge amounts of time that I can use for more important things.

The Internet has also revolutionised the world's economy. It has opened doors to careers that did not exist twenty years ago and has created companies that solely exist online. What would we do without Amazon and Ebay? In just over a decade Google has not just only become a household name but it is also a multibillion pound corporation.

Yet for all the positives there is a negative side to the internet. Such has been the advent of the Internet that organisations that were once established institutions have been cast aside as irrelevant. Who would have thought that the good old fashioned library and the age old book store would face extinction?

The old fashioned letter that has been around for hundreds of years has been dramatically reduced in number. After all, who wants to wait a day for information when they can have it in seconds?

Daily newspaper circulations have also decreased in number over the last few years as people catch up on the news over the World Wide Web.

## THE DOWNSIDE TO THE INTERNET

It is in regard to the negative aspect of the Internet why this chapter is written. Now you can hold your horses, I'm not saying that not having the Internet is a part of the standards we have for ministry.

But I have stressed before what matters more than the standards is the spirit of those standards. The issue is about righteousness, exampleship and having impact for the kingdom of God. Though there is much to be thankful about the Internet there is also a very dark side that if we expose ourselves to it has serious ramifications.

It may be a shame that with the coming of the Internet we have seen the gradual decrease in libraries, newspapers and book stores. As sad as this may seem we need to recognise that this is simply one of those things that progress brings. As one thing comes it replaces another. This is how life has played out for centuries.

There was a time when transistor radios were all the rage. For the first time it was possible for the radio to be portable. It was a landmark invention. I can remember people in the 1970s carrying their little transistor radio listening to the football, catching up on the news or listening to music.

But by the late 1970s the transistor radio along with the eight track cartridge were replaced by the cassette deck and the release of the Sony "Walkman". The "Walkman" and its clones survived for only ten years or so when the CD came out and we know that CDs today are struggling with the arrival of the MP3.

The same is true with the Internet. Yes it is sad that the bookstore as we know it is phasing out but such is the transient nature of life that we call progress. It is the passing of one type of practical application to another. It is neither moral nor spiritual in nature.

What is dangerous about the Internet in context to Christianity is that it exposes Christians to spiritual dangers that never existed or were highly restricted even twenty years ago. These are dangers that are destroying many Christians' relationship with God, ruining their testimonies and breaking up Christian homes and marriages.

Anything that can do so much damage ought to be looked at carefully and with much thoroughness. We ought not to let the wonderful benefits of the Web so entice us that we lose our ability to reason and to inspect things cautiously and wisely.

## THE SNARE OF PORNOGRAPHY

Right off the bat we need to understand that the Internet is the biggest gateway to pornography. It doesn't take a genius to figure out that pornography is mental fornication.

Consider the fact that sex is the number one search topic on the Internet. Consider that there are currently more than 372 million pornographic websites available on the Internet. Consider that over 100,000 websites allow illegal child pornography. Consider that the average age of first Internet exposure to pornography is eleven years old. Consider that 2.5 billion emails a day are pornographic in nature. Consider that 70% of men between the ages of 18 and 34 visit pornographic websites in a typical month. Consider that boys between the ages of 12 and 17 are the largest consumers of pornography and that 90% of them view online porn while doing their homework. Consider that every second more than US$3,076 is being spent on pornography. Consider that every second 28,250 Internet users are viewing pornography. Consider that the worldwide internet sex industry for 2006 is more than US$97 billion which is more revenue than Microsoft, Google, EBay, Apple and Yahoo combined.

That's a whole lot of things to consider.

There was a time where pornography was considered the realm of perverts. Twenty years or so ago you could only find it in brown paper bags at the top shelf in the newsagents. But because of the Internet pornography has become instantly accessible the viewer doesn't have to risk shame in asking for the magazine on the top shelf. Not just that but pornography over the Internet is free and no one has to know you are an addict.

As tragic as those statistics are what's worse is the fact that pornography has infiltrated the church. One statistic I read said that 51% of pastors admit that looking at internet pornography is a possible temptation with 37% saying that it is a current struggle.[5] In a 2000 Christianity Today survey, 33% of clergy admitted to visiting a sexually explicit website and of those who had visited such a sight 53% had visited such sites a few times in the past year and

---

[5] Christianity Today, Leadership Survey, 12/2001

18% visit explicit sites between a couple times a month and once a week.

In November 2002, the American Academy of Matrimonial Lawyers, an organisation that consisted of the nation's top divorce and matrimonial law attorneys, met in Chicago, Illinois. An informal survey was conducted in regards to the impact of the Internet on marriages. Of the 350 attendees, 62% said that the Internet played a significant factor in the divorce cases they had handled in the year 2000.

They also admitted that:

68% of the divorce cases involved one party meeting a new love interest over the Internet;

56% of the divorce cases involved one party having an obsessive interest in pornographic websites;

47% of the divorce cases involved one party spending excessive time on the computer;

33% of the divorce cases cited excessive time communicating in sexualised chat rooms or forums.

I have mentioned these statistics in the hope of making you realise just how powerful the Internet can be to bring harm to people's spiritual lives. Pornography eats away at your spiritual life like termites take to wood. You underestimate its power at your own peril.

Too many Christians overlook the potential Pandora's Box of the Internet and their own sinful nature. All it takes is for you to be spiritually fatigued or vulnerable and have instant access to the Internet for you to open a door that will eventually destroy not only your spiritual life but your testimony and even your family.

I have spoken to many men over the years that have backslidden and ended up separated or divorced because of this unspeakable addiction.

It is therefore recommended by our Fellowship that you put up an internet filter on your computer. These internet filters or web blockers are programs that will prevent you from accessing internet porn sites and in the majority of cases stop pornographic pop-up ads from infiltrating your computer.

From time to time these filters will block legitimate websites and for that reason there is a password given that can unlock the website that is blocked. This password should be given to a trusted friend or family member that you are accountable to or to a spouse. This password should only be known by that person and if you are hindered from accessing a legitimate website that person can tap the password in and give you access.

It may seem time consuming but it is better to be safe than sorry. Maybe for 99% of the time we are completely in control but there will come a time when you will be glad you have no access to these pages as it would have saved your ministry, your testimony and possibly your family.

## MOMMY ALWAYS TOLD ME NEVER TO TALK TO STRANGERS

There are other dangers on the Internet besides pornography. There is much to be said about these dangers, so much so that an entire book could be written about it. Because this is simply a chapter and not a book I cannot go into it in its entirety but limit these dangers to the most important.

It is possible that these websites are more

dangerous than pornography because they seem to be less sinister. The dangers lie in their subtlety and the truth be known subtle dangers are far more dangerous than the ones in the open.

The most dangerous of these is perhaps social networking websites. Sure, the Internet can be a place where you can get in contact with long lost friends and relatives but the downside is communicating and making friendships with people that you don't know in the slightest.

I am sure that every one of us growing up as children was taught never to talk to strangers. Whether on the street or in the bus or in the playground we kept ourselves away from people we did not know. Yet on the Internet we without hesitation get into conversation with completely unfamiliar people.

It is either naivety or more than likely that we switch off common sense and reason and talk to people we don't know and just accept that they are who they say they are. Amazing!

It is staggering how many people who, in an Internet chat room, believe that John Smith, a 32 year old single white male from London who works as a graphic designer is in fact John Smith, a 32 year old single white male from London who works as a graphics designer.

Here is a tragic but true tale written to the Nigerian Tribune:

*"I am an American married to a Nigerian. I met him via the **Internet**. Six months after our on-line meeting, we got married. The wedding took place in Lagos two months ago. I have since discovered that I have been deceived in so many ways. For instance, he said he was 29 years of age whereas he was 22.*

*He claimed to be a football player when he was in fact unemployed. He also claimed to have travelled all over Europe when his passport doesn't even have a single entry. I am not sure the passport that he provided for my visa was even a valid document. During my visit to Nigeria, I discovered that the man drinks like a fish, hangs out in bars and is a chain smoker. Prior to the wedding, he kept me isolated from his friends, I didn't get to me them until we got to the reception. They were also a bunch of swearing beer- drinking men. After the wedding, I returned home very depressed about the situation. Almost immediately, I began to receive despondent calls from my husband with one life threatening crisis or another that required me to wire monies. When I refused to send money and challenged him, he became verbally abusive and threatened violence against me if I did not comply. I still refused and he told me I was an unfit wife for not trusting him. I then began a research divorce or annulment options."*

It would almost seem laughable if it weren't so tragic and although reports like this are a dime a dozen the reality is that there are new victims every day.

As bad as that story is, it could be worse. She could have met her murderer and not just a con artist. How many innocent young girls have gone to meet what they think of is a teenage young boy only to find out when it is too late that he is a registered paedophile.

On the 24th of October 2009, seventeen year old Ashleigh Hall went missing from her home in Darlington, County Durham. She was found dead the following Monday night murdered by a registered sex offender by the name of Peter Chapman who met her on Facebook pretending to be a sixteen year old boy.

I read of a sting operation done in the USA by the FBI where they got a policewoman to infiltrate a chat-room for girls by pretending to be a sixteen year old girl. The discovered that the twenty two other girls in the chat room were in fact guys looking for teenage girls to chat up.

Yet for all of this, it is tragic to see in the church vulnerable and lonely young women taking off and leaving Christ for the sake of a man she met on the Internet. When you try and talk her out of it she tells you that he is for real. He is saved, living for Jesus, has a heart for God, working a good job and wants to marry her. He wants to do this all by meeting you on Facebook.

I have seen young ladies run off only to face serious heartbreak in the end. One young lady I know ran off to America to marry a man she met on the Internet. After years of physical and verbal abuse she desperately wants to return back to Britain.

## THE BREEDING GROUND OF NARCISSISM

This is not only the scourge of young women only but many men as well have fallen to the trap of the internet dating website or chat rooms? A man may have gone on a website where he is reacquainted with old friends including his old girlfriend in high school. Nostalgia floods in as he remembers the good old days and so he leaves his wife and family in an attempt to restore the feel good factor of having his first 'true' love.

Why is so easy for people, one after the other, to be falling into the same trap. I guess they don't call the Internet the Web for nothing.

In an article written in the Daily Telegraph dated the 2nd of October 2009, Professor Mark Griffiths of the Nottingham Trent University made the point that *"The internet is a dis-inhibiting medium, where people's emotional guard is down. It's the same phenomenon as meeting a stranger on the train, where you find yourself telling your life story to someone you don't know, something you wouldn't have dreamed of doing in your local pub. The internet feels anonymous, safe and non-threatening – even if it isn't. People are more trusting and form deep attachments – hence concerns about young people using chat-rooms, where they can fall prey to adult agendas...People fall in love much quicker online generally than in real life, because they reveal more of themselves on a very personal level much sooner than they would face to face."*

It makes sense and it goes in explaining why although people know better, every now and again someone in church will fall spiritually by meeting someone on the Web by giving their hearts to someone they really don't know and when the trap is sprung everything unravels.

The ancient book of Proverbs written thousands of years ago gives a great remedy for such dilemmas. Proverbs 12:26 states, *"The righteous should choose his friends carefully, for the way of the wicked leads them astray."* There is nothing careful about talking to people on the Internet.

Andrea Hall, the mother of Ashleigh Hall (who I mentioned before) stated in an article in the Daily Mail that *"I can't blame the internet, but it is about time that somebody looked at ways of introducing controls which stops people putting up false pictures and false information. She had about 400 friends on Facebook and knew every single one of them. We can't imagine how she got to be friends with someone she didn't know. She made one mistake and has paid for it with her life. It's not Ashleigh's fault what happened. All we can do as parents is to try and get across to them that there are two sides to the internet."*

I do feel sorry for Andrea but she is either naive or deceived. The fact that her daughter met up with the paedophile shows she did not know every single one of her four hundred friends. Four hundred friends! Who on earth has four hundred friends and how can you possibly know four hundred people properly?

But that is the issue. It is impossible to know all these 'friends' and as Christians the Bible says that we should choose them carefully.

The Hebrew word that is translated 'carefully' is used only twenty three times in the Old Testament. Of those twenty three occasions, fifteen times it speak of the twelve spies searching out the Promised Land. The Hebrew word means a thorough examination, to spy out and to explore.

If that is the case, how many of our friends have we thoroughly examined? How can a seventeen year old successfully examine her four hundred friends properly? It is absolutely impossible.

Social network websites like Facebook feeds our vanity as we deceive ourselves into thinking we have more friends than we really have. Our narcissism opens the door to exploitation by forces outside of our control.

What makes the Internet a dangerous place is that it feeds our ego and we are completely unaware of it. It flatters us by making us seem more important than we really are. We are unconscious of the subtle pride slowly growing inside us as we add friend to friend on our Facebook page and before you know it you are caught up in egotism and self-importance.

Consider the rapid growth of Twitter where one of the goals is to get as many 'followers' as you can. It is sad to hear of people tweeting and letting others know that they have left the restaurant or they are going to get a haircut. Who cares? This is plain old self-indulgence.

# A MAJOR CAUSE OF DISTRACTION

If pride and ego are not bad enough consider that the world of the Internet is today's major source of distraction. We are so busy talking to friends on Facebook and Tweeting our whereabouts to strangers that we have less time to do more important things.

People spend hours on the Internet 'surfing' the net and talking to 'friends' that they have no time to read their bibles, pray, go to a real fellowship and sit amongst real people or to add something beneficial to their lives. The times we spend surfing the net and doing nothing we could have spent learning an instrument or getting a qualification.

Without going over what I spoke about regarding television and music the Internet steals away our precious time, time that we can never replace. How much could have been accomplished for good if we were not so distracted? How much more spiritual we could have been if we were not diverted from godliness? How many things we could have done quicker and better if we did not lack focus?

The irony of the Internet is that it was created to make us smarter but in reality it has made us dumber. It was meant to improve our lives, not worsen it. It was meant to help us save precious hours by cutting down the times it took to do things but now it has caused us to lose precious hours as we are distracted by the various things we can do on it.

British based American psychologist Dr Aric Sigman points out that the amount of time we spend with each other has slumped dramatically with the advent of Facebook and other social networking websites.

Not only that but as a result of the Internet we are damaging our health as our devotion to such websites could alter the way genes work, upset immune responses, hormone levels and the function of arteries and influence mental performance. Dr Sigman adds, *"Social networking sites should allow us to embellish our social lives, but what we find is very different. The tail is wagging the dog. These are not the tools that enhance, they are the tools that displace."*

His advice is that we "get off Facebook and get a life".[6] I agree.

I personally think that the Internet is a greater danger to Christianity than the television and as Christians we must be vigilant in our attitude towards it. The apostle Paul stated very clearly in Ephesians 5:15-17 stating, *"See then that you walk circumspectly, not as fools but as wise, redeeming the time, because the days are evil. Therefore do not be unwise, but understand what the will of the Lord is."*

Let us remember that another term for the Internet is the World Wide Web. I believe the meaning of the term was that various people from around the world could load their learning in one place so that the common knowledge could be accessed by all.

Yet the word 'web' reminds me of the spider's snare in which unsuspecting victims are lured to their doom. We would be wise to remember that.

In closing, that reminds me of a poem I heard long ago as a little boy. It is called "The Spider and the Fly" and it was written by Mary Howitt in 1829.

---

[6] http://uk.news.yahoo.com/4/20090219/tuk-get-off-facebook-and-get-a-life-dba1618.html

## THE SPIDER AND THE FLY

"Will you walk into my parlour?" said the Spider to the Fly, "Tis the prettiest little parlour that ever you did spy; The way into my parlour is up a winding stair, And I have many curious things to show you when you are there."

"Oh no, no," said the Fly, "to ask me is in vain; For who goes up your winding stair can ne'er come down again."

"I'm sure you must be weary, dear, with soaring up so high; Will you rest upon my little bed?" said the Spider to the Fly. "There are pretty curtains drawn around, the sheets are fine and thin; And if you like to rest awhile, I'll snugly tuck you in!"

"Oh no, no," said the little Fly, "for I've often heard it said They never, never wake again, who sleep upon your bed!"

Said the cunning Spider to the Fly, "Dear friend, what can I do To prove that warm affection I've always felt for you? I have within my pantry, good store of all that's nice; I'm sure you're very welcome - will you please take a slice?"

"Oh no, no," said the little Fly, "kind sir, that cannot be, I've heard what's in your pantry, and I do not wish to see!"

"Sweet creature," said the Spider, "you're witty and you're wise; How handsome are your gauzy wings, how brilliant are your eyes! I have a little looking-glass upon my parlor shelf; If you step in one moment, dear, you shall behold yourself."

"I thank you, gentle sir," she said, "for what you're

pleased to say; And bidding good morning now, I'll call another day."

The Spider turned him round about, and went into his den, For well he knew the silly Fly would soon come back again; So he wove a subtle web in a little corner sly, And set his table ready to dine upon the Fly. Then he came out to his door again, and merrily did sing, "Come hither, hither, pretty Fly, with the pearl and silver wing; Your robes are green and purple, there's a crest upon your head; Your eyes are like the diamond bright, but mine are as dull as lead."

Alas, alas! how very soon this silly little Fly, Hearing his wily, flattering words, came slowly flitting by; With buzzing wings she hung aloft, then near and nearer drew, Thinking only of her brilliant eyes, and green and purple hue; Thinking only of her crested head - poor foolish thing! At last, Up jumped the cunning Spider, and fiercely held her fast. He dragged her up his winding stair, into his dismal den Within his little parlor - but she ne'er came out again!

And now, dear little children, who may this story read, To idle, silly, flattering words, I pray you ne'er heed; Unto an evil counsellor close heart, and ear, and eye, And take a lesson from this tale of the Spider and the Fly.

As Stan Lee would put it...'Nuff said!'

## ABOUT THE AUTHOR

Jay Nembhard has been pastoring for seventeen years in the Christian Fellowship Ministries. Originally from the Potter's House Church in South London, he has pioneered churches in Manchester and Wolverhampton, England and is currently a missionary in Mandeville, Jamaica. He is married to Cheryl and the father of two boys and a girl.

OTHER TITLES AVAILABLE FROM YOUR FAVORITE BOOKSTORE:

*Twice Dead: The True Death and Life Story of Roman Gutierrez*
By David J. Drum
ISBN: 978-0-9856041-0-3
When Roman Gutierrez was eleven years old, his father died from a heroin overdose. Roman resolved, in his anger and his pain, that someday God would take him the same way. He became an addict, a year later he went to juvenile detention for stealing, and attempted suicide the year after that. At fifteen he got into a fight and was pronounced dead for six minutes. At nineteen he was stabbed by his best friend, and pronounced dead for five minutes. When Roman was twenty-five, he shot up all the heroin he had so his torment would end ... and realized he didn't want to die. That's when a miracle occurred... (for more info visit www.TwiceDeadMinistries.com)

*Still Taking the Land*
By David J. Drum
ISBN: 978-0-9817634-9-1
The Christian Fellowship Ministries (CFM) began as the humble desire of Pastor Wayman Mitchell to put into practice the principles of discipleship, evangelism, and church planting outlined in the Holy Bible. After forty years of obedience to Christ's Great Commission, there are more than 1,800 CFM churches in 125 countries, with an ever-increasing number of new churches being planted each year. This volume presents the practical experience of Pastors Wayman and Greg Mitchell, especially the Biblical principles that have guided CFM growth. Included are essential guidelines of church planting ranging from hands-on application to those of a spiritual nature, as well as a firsthand interview with straight answers to important questions for both those who feel the call of God to enter the ministry and those pastors who are raising up and sending out new workers. For more info visit www.davidjdrum.com)

*Offering Stories, Quotes, and Illustrations Volume 1*
**By Robert Polaco**
ISBN: 978-0-9817634-5-3
Volume 1 is a compilation of over 200 offering stories, quotes, and illustrations. Each illustration also contains a note line where pastors or administrators can indicate the date on which the illustration was used, preventing the potential embarrassment of reusing an illustration. This is a must have companion for any pastor or church administrator.

*Offering Stories, Quotes, and Illustrations Volume 2*
**By Robert Polaco**
ISBN: 978-0-9817634-7-7
Volume 2 is the anticipated sequel in Robert Polaco's compilation series, and includes 375 new entries organized with descriptive titles. This is a must have companion for any pastor or church administrator, filled with illustrations that inspire people to liberality. These illustrations often include supporting scriptural references, and each entry includes a line where one can choose to write in where or when it was used.

*Freedom To Choose*
**By E. L. Kidwell**
ISBN: 978-0-9817634-1-5
Visit the Kingdom of Heaven before Earth was created. Enter the throne room of God, and experience the events before time began. Discover the secrets of why hell's chief accuser betrayed the love and perfection of His Creator, and set himself to destroy the race of mankind in seething hatred. Enjoy this thought-provoking drama as it brings to life the Genesis account of the Bible.

Printed in Great Britain
by Amazon